The Medical Library Association Guide to Answering Questions about the Affordable Care Act

Medical Library Association Books

The Medical Library Association (MLA) features books that showcase the expertise of health sciences librarians for other librarians and professionals. MLA Books are excellent resources for librarians in hospitals, medical research practice, and other settings. These volumes will provide health care professionals and patients with accurate information that can improve outcomes and save lives. Each book in the series has been overseen editorially since conception by the Medical Library Association Books Panel, composed of MLA members with expertise spanning the breadth of health sciences librarianship.

Medical Library Association Books Panel

About the Medical Library Association

Founded in 1898, MLA is a 501(c)(3) nonprofit, educational organization of 4,000 individual and institutional members in the health sciences information field that provides lifelong educational opportunities, supports a knowledgebase of health information research, and works with a global network of partners to promote the importance of quality information for improved health to the health care community and the public.

Books in Series

The Medical Library Association Guide to Answering Questions about the Affordable Care Act

Edited by Emily Vardell

ROWMAN & LITTLEFIELD
Lanham • Boulder • New York • London

Published by Rowman & Littlefield
A wholly owned subsidiary of The Rowman & Littlefield Publishing Group, Inc.
4501 Forbes Boulevard, Suite 200, Lanham, Maryland 20706
www.rowman.com

Unit A, Whitacre Mews, 26-34 Stannary Street, London SE11 4AB

British Library Cataloguing in Publication Information Available

Library of Congress Cataloging-in-Publication Data

The Medical Library Association guide to answering questions about the Affordable Care Act /
edited by Emily Vardell.
p. cm. — (Medical Library Association books)
Includes bibliographical references and index.
ISBN 978-1-4422-5536-4 (hardcover : alk. paper) — ISBN 978-1-4422-5537-1 (pbk. : alk. paper) —
ISBN 978-1-4422-5538-8 (ebook)
I. Vardell, Emily, 1983– , editor. II. Medical Library Association, issuing body. III. Title: Guide to
answering questions about the Affordable Care Act. IV. Series: Medical Library Association books.
[DNLM: 1. United States. Patient Protection and Affordable Care Act. 2. Insurance, Health—United
States. 3. Legislation as Topic—United States. 4. Libraries, Medical—United States. 5. Library
Services—United States. W 275 AA1]
RA412.2
368.38'200973—dc23
2015021293

♾ ™ The paper used in this publication meets the minimum requirements of American
National Standard for Information Sciences Permanence of Paper for Printed Library
Materials, ANSI/NISO Z39.48-1992.

Printed in the United States of America

To all the information professionals providing
quality health insurance information on the front lines

Contents

Introduction

Following the passage and implementation of the Affordable Care Act (ACA), librarians are more frequently called upon to provide assistance with navigating the health insurance marketplace and understanding health insurance terminology and forms. Libraries offer an ideal context for health insurance information seeking, as librarians have traditionally assisted with completing public assistance forms and are well trained in ascertaining and meeting information needs. President Barack Obama recognized this national resource when he requested help from librarians in assisting the public with this new phase of health insurance in the United States during his call to action at the 2013 American Library Association Conference.

The Medical Library Association Guide to Answering Questions about the Affordable Care Act is designed to serve as a practical guide for librarians seeking to learn more about the ACA; locate authoritative, nonbiased information regarding the ACA; and serve patrons searching for ACA information for personal or research purposes. While the book focuses specifically on the unique role that health sciences librarians play in serving the general public as well as health care providers, biomedical researchers, and health sciences students, the book also contains guidance relevant to any information professional working with ACA information.

Tailored for a librarian audience, the book begins with a general introduction to the Affordable Care Act, highlighting the aspects of the ACA legislation most pertinent to librarians. In chapter 1 Francisca Goldsmith traces a brief history of health care reform in the United States, setting the stage for the passage and politics of the ACA. The chapter also pulls out specific aspects of the ACA that may not be as familiar with readers, including the impact on Medicare beneficiaries, the increased emphasis on preventative care, and the consequences for health care information systems.

In chapter 2 Margot Malachowski builds on this foundation by focusing on the role of the librarian in relation to ACA implementation. This chapter is of relevance to librarians working in many kinds of information settings. Specific settings discussed in depth include hospital information management, academic assignments and research (supported by LibGuides and other information portals), and formal instruction (to multiple audiences, from students to health care providers). Malachowski outlines specific opportunities for targeted efforts that address ACA information technology mandates as well as consumer information needs. The chapter concludes with a discussion of the role librarians can play in the public library setting, and the steps that all librarians can take to document the benefits they provide to their respective communities.

Chapter 3, the chapter I wrote on health insurance literacy, provides a foundation for those seeking to familiarize themselves with research on individuals' understanding of health insurance concepts. The research presented in that chapter assists librarians in making evidence-based decisions regarding services and projects they may wish to undertake to address health insurance and ACA information needs. In an age of budget cuts and limited staffing, it is imperative that librarians review relevant research and allocate resources to initiatives that are supported by the most recent evidence.

Chapter 4 continues these connections, discussing how a librarian can break down an ACA question, including a step-by-step guide. Deborah H. Charbonneau and Kelli Ham include a discussion of general guidelines for health insurance reference, the steps necessary to ascertain and digest the information need, opportunities for staff training, and the emotional aspects of this kind of sensitive reference work. Their suggestions and guidelines are explained in a helpful checklist form, enabling librarians to implement these ideas in their own institutions. While the chapter focuses on the health insurance information need, Charbonneau and Ham's suggested strategies are applicative in a host of health sciences reference settings.

The next part of the book focuses on trends in ACA and health insurance information provision. These chapters are designed to serve as springboards for those librarians interested in learning best practices and recommendations. The discussion begins in chapter 5 with original research I conducted to explore the types of ACA information services librarians are providing. These nationwide trends are presented to demonstrate what librarians are currently doing and bring attention to areas where librarians could be doing more (e.g., obtaining ACA-related training, proactively marketing services, etc.).

Next, I highlight librarians as best-practice profiles in chapter 6 to articulate the types of information services provided by health sciences librarians responding to ACA information needs. The profiles in the chapter include information mediator, programming host, research support, presentation support, embedded clinical support, and librarian advocate. These specific, real-life examples demonstrate how librarians are taking on this work within their job responsibilities and may provide ideas of how other librarians can undertake new projects and initiatives in this arena.

The final chapters 7 and 8 contain authoritative lists of recommended, unbiased ACA resources for consumers and practitioners. These annotated bibliographies by Kelli Ham, Michele Malloy, and Brenda Linares are excellent places for librarians to familiarize themselves with ACA logistical information as well as locate authoritative resources on insurance terminology. As librarians are increasingly being called upon to address health insurance information needs from the general public as well as researchers, these chapters provide concrete, helpful advice in locating quality information resources to support the provision of unbiased, evidence-based answers.

The Medical Library Association Guide to Answering Questions about the Affordable Care Act is designed to be a practical tool that librarians can directly apply to their work. This book presents the latest research in this area and interweaves evidence-based suggestions for getting the most benefit out of an investment of time, energy, and money. Librarians and information professionals are encouraged to review the checklists, profiles, and recommended resources provided in this book and select those tips that are most relevant for their particular information setting.

The Medical Library Association (MLA) has a strong tradition of educating librarians and addressing cutting-edge information needs. Librarians are uniquely poised to provide assistance with Affordable Care Act research, implementation, and individual needs. In addressing many of the multiple issues at the crossroads of library science and Affordable Care Act information needs, this MLA series book is written as a practical guide and tool to support these efforts and inspire new directions.

Chapter One

Overview of the Affordable Care Act

*Historical Context and Knowledge Management
Concerns*

Francisca Goldsmith

In March 2010, a federal bill was signed into law that has become popularly known as the Affordable Care Act. In this overview, I will place the Act into historical context, note the rollout stages it encompasses, and point out how its details precipitate knowledge management concerns with which American librarians need to engage.

The Act is federal legislation, which means that it governs aspects of the national insurance, medical, pharmaceutical, health care education, and allied industries; personal legal responsibility; access to government support services; and other areas of the lives of practitioners, taxpayers, human resources planners, and social service providers. It is, as a matter of course given its parameters, complex. However, it comprises logical parts and can be grasped both through those parts and as a positioning document. In this way it is akin to legislation that may seem quite familiar, such as the large suite of laws and regulations governing employment practices and activities or the Americans with Disabilities Act. Just as these two established legal areas each comprise aspects of rights, responsibilities, and practical and financial concerns, so this Act, too, touches a variety of concerns, service structures, and agency regulations that come into play.

In order to meet the information and knowledge management challenges such a complexity presents, deconstructing the Act's goals and strategies offers a grounded understanding of the who, what, why, how, and when of the Act's unfolding. While you almost certainly have personal opinions about the politics involved in the Act's creation and maintenance, understanding the Act's contextualizing history and requirements should be free of the bias of political opinion. Instead of attending to your personal sense of right and wrong, I invite you to turn toward the facts with which we have to work in connecting the law to those who look to librarians for pathfinding.

AMERICAN HEALTH CARE, HEALTH INSURANCE, AND THE CENTURY PREDATING THE AFFORDABLE CARE ACT

Dating from Theodore Roosevelt's failed campaign against Woodrow Wilson in the 1912 presidential election, U.S. presidents (and candidates) have developed plans for addressing the nation's need for accessible health care. With a medical establishment that developed alongside a fee-for-service model and third-party payment of those fees, a variety of factors have long informed both medical practice and health care planning in the public sphere.

The 1935 passage of the Social Security Act, during Franklin Delano Roosevelt's presidency, included the recognition of the reality that acquiring savings sufficient for emergencies, let alone sufficient for investment and the growth of personal wealth, falls outside the capacity of many Americans. Thirty years later, the aspects of care expenditures related specifically to health and health care received attention in President Johnson's signing of Social Security amendments that introduced the Medicare and Medicaid programs. These programs place the federal government as the gatekeeper for health care access for specific populations deemed at risk, due to age or poverty, from the high cost of private medical care.

Concern about the costs of health care continued to attract leadership attention in both political parties. In 1974, President Nixon called for national health care of some sort, noting that more than twenty-five million Americans (in a population then numbering under 215 million) lacked insurance, even with Medicare and Medicaid in place. The lobby opposing any such easement at that time was led by the American Medical Association.

During ensuing decades, every sitting president achieved some reform of the industrial medical care structure, whether these were adjustments to Medicare and Medicaid regulations or ensuring access for all to public hospital emergency rooms. (Later in this section, I look at how overreliance on emergency care itself adds to the librarian's need to reeducate health care consumers). President Obama's model for the Affordable Care Act drew heavily on the work and policy development that occurred in Massachusetts with the 2006 passage of a mandate requiring universal access to "affordable, quality, accountable health care" (Commonwealth of Massachusetts 2006). The Massachusetts law was developed under a Republican governor, Mitt Romney.

While individual physicians and clinicians, like everyone else, may hold personal political opinions that differ from the course of history that has brought the federal Affordable Care Act into law, the American Medical Association ceased to operate in the role of antagonist when the bill's passage was undergoing lobbying pressures. Instead, the insurance industry became the paramount lobbying group to address. At the time of the Affordable Care Act's passage in 2010, forty-five million Americans lacked health insurance of any kind. The insurance industry had become a significant force not only in matters of payment, but also in gatekeeping such areas of health care as ongoing access for those with preexisting health conditions, preventive care access, and development of subject pools for clinical trials. To gain the support of this increasingly powerful player in the connection between patient and health care provider, considerable political work had to be done.

In addition to the regulatory changes the Act introduced to insurers and others holding financial interest in the American fee-for-service health care model, the Act also brought attention to the generation of Americans who had developed emergency-room dependency as their only contact with health care. By mandating free access to preventive care, the Affordable Care Act asserts an enormous change in orientation of those who have been trained to view health care as symptom relief rather than health maintenance. This reorientation calls upon librarians as well as direct health care providers to engage in the public education and reeducation process that aligns with preventive health care and health maintenance orientations and away from self-diagnosed needs to seek medical attention (Fleming 2010).

OVERVIEW OF THE FORMAL ACT

The Patient Protection and Affordable Care Act, as the legislation is formally named, targets a number of goals and employs strategies that are phased in across nearly a decade.[1] These strategies can be threaded along four themes related to health and health care:

- Patients' rights
- Personal responsibilities (including tax-related matters)
- Employer responsibilities
- Health care delivery improvements

The Act's various mandates address how insurance companies may and may not control access to services, how the health care workforce must be expanded, hospital performance measures, and tax-based credits and penalties as monetary pressures for following the law. Because of the breadth of these concerns, many federal departments are directly involved in both rule construction and oversight. In addition, each state has the right to further expand (but not constrict) the Affordable Care Act's strategic alignments; thus, state-level government agencies may have local rules that residents, businesses, and health care providers working in the state are required to follow in addition to federal rules.

Even before we layer on the realities of political opinion, communication challenges related to native language, literacy levels, and technology lapses, the mandates related to the Act obviously call for complex knowledge management skills. As librarians, that complexity must be extended still further to account for our professional commitment to providing others with clarity about matters of fact.

In the following three sections of this chapter, I consider the dynamics of three areas of concern addressed by the Act that require knowledge leadership for many who are required to respond to the Act's mandates. Such leadership requires that we first organize our own knowledge and awareness of relevant resources, and then make our information management skills available to the community we serve. While I refer to "knowledge management" in this chapter, included in this scope are all public service library staff involved with guiding their communities in managing the knowledge sets related to this complex Act.

HEALTH INSURANCE, MEDICARE, AND MEDICAID

Because the Act reifies the third-party payment of fees for health care services provided, understanding how health insurance works from an economic as well as an individual coverage viewpoint is necessary. For the millions who are now legally responsible for acquiring health insurance—either for themselves and their family or for their employees—the personal financial literacy learning curve may be steep. Selecting a health insurance plan requires one to have a realistic sense of current health care needs; understand the operative natures of co-pays, premiums, co-insurance, and other numerical data points; and make choices that are in some ways philosophical, such as determining whether a health maintenance organization or a preferred provider network is better suited to one's health care beliefs (refer to chapter 3 of this book for further discussion of health insurance literacy).

Medicare and Medicaid are actually federal subsidized insurance programs themselves. The Affordable Care Act ties access to Medicaid (which goes by different names in some states' administrations of these federal funds) to the same "marketplace" registration and administration machinery from which private insurers are operating. This does not mean that clients of Medicare and Medicaid can practice choice among the insurers, but it does mean that they must now enter the health care coverage stream just as those making independent choices of insurers do: via a database that is localized enough to account for cost-of-living differentials by region and is national in scope when considering Internal Revenue Service implications.

At least at this time, clients covered by Medicare cannot shop outside the Medicare-approved network of health care providers. Social service staff work as links between the health insurance marketplace's computer interface and Medicare/Medicaid clients. However, Americans who previously did not qualify for such cost supports now may do so (Henry J. Kaiser Family Foundation 2012) and may well need assistance in accessing their state marketplace—or social services office—due to limited language or literacy, inexperience with computer registration programs, and other concerns.

Failure to attain health insurance coverage becomes increasingly penalized, in taxation terms, across ensuing years. At the same time, overbuying is also discouraged through tax penalties. "Cadillac policy" is the term employed in government regulations to describe such overbroad, and commensurately overpriced, insurance plans that free the well-to-do policyholder from responsible use of health care resources. For example, a Cadillac policy might pay for on-demand (and professionally unwarranted) cosmetic surgery. For the best off in the country, this also presents something to learn: that overbuying health insurance will not be tolerated without tax penalty is a concept that may strike some as unimagined and thus requires, even where literacy may be presumed as superior, information sharing of the Act's stipulations. Librarians have an opportunity to inform community members of all socioeconomic levels and insurance coverage types of the impact that the Act may have on their taxes and other financial interests.

Of significant benefit to a national population who must learn about these complex matters is the federal government's own self-implicated mandate that "plain language" be used in web-based communication.[2] In librarians' knowledge management work related to the Affordable Care Act, subscribing to the Plain Language Initiative's parameters can take us far toward meeting local knowledge needs.

CHANGING HEALTH CARE EMPHASES

The Affordable Care Act specifically calls out preventive care as a value. Further, the Act addresses hospital performance measures as well as mental health needs and care, substance addiction rehabilitation as a medical process, and pediatric dental and vision care needs. In these areas, the Act affects the social construct of what "health care" means. Educating the general population to recognize their new rights to recovery treatments, prophylactic medications, and children's vision care suggests many possible touch points between traditional information services and family-targeted programming. Even behavioral rules for public buildings such as libraries may need to be reexamined in light of new rights expressed in the law. For example, slovenly dress or delusional speech are often termed library behavioral code violations and may lead to the summoning of law enforcement to cope with infractions. Now these signs of mental illness may require librarians to learn what health-based service in the community is the more appropriate agency to call.

Rather than seeing these complexities as irksome, I suggest that they open many attractive new opportunities to refine community engagement and thereby support community health. However, the first step needs to be a clear understanding of the Act's dimensions as well as its scheduled rollout. To get a clear calendar of when different elements of the Act come into force, you can refer to the federal government's "Key Features of the Affordable Care Act by Year" (http://www.hhs.gov/healthcare/facts/timeline/timeline-text.html). Of course, it helps to plan ahead when it comes to developing programs to alert your community to impending changes!

ALTERING THE MEDICAL DELIVERY SYSTEM

The Act also addresses such industry-specific details as how records are maintained and where clinicians need to practice. While these are stipulated within the Act, there are additional developments likely to arise as extrapolations of law into practice. How changes in access to health care—and to health insurance—color social expectations of health care and its availability will further inform medical practice evolution.

Clinical trials, for example, are likely to evolve as the body of potential test subjects becomes more diverse. Greater access to affordable resources for substance recovery assumes more will both seek out such programs and succeed in completing them. Eventually, young adults who are in foster care from a threshold period prior to their eighteenth birthdays will have access to both preventive and paid ameliorative health care between the time they turn eighteen and when they reach twenty-six, a currently ignored societal need.[3] Each of these examples illustrates how changes in health care access primes a population for changes in employability, civic engagement, and living standards' expectations.

With government subsidies and tax relief programs keyed to income in increased and more effective manners through the Act, a larger segment of the population can explore health care coverage, seek health care, and investigate tax relief for health care expenditures. All these concerns touch information access, of course, and so speak to the need for proactive public education and information support.

LAWS EVOLVE

The political nature of the Affordable Care Act is not unique, either to the enacted version or to the history of health care access laws. Community members who gather their information from news sources, neighbors, and family members are likely to confuse politics with current fact. At this time, the Act is in force as passed and amended, and Americans uncertain of the law's "sticking power" may need the guidance of information specialists to work between opinion and enforceable current law. For the information specialist, this means keeping abreast of changes in law, as well as of community information needs and access points. Librarians must develop the capacity to distinguish among types of information in order to provide fact-based and relevant information leadership. This implicates information service delivery staff in the ethical requirement to attain new knowledge and continue to train and develop professionally (American Library Association 2008).

With more than a century of social, economic, professional, and political developments leading to the current Act, what is needed now in the library community is responsive information sharing, rather than reactive or selective dispersal of future forecasting. The fact that multiple federal, and in many cases state, agencies are writing regulations that follow from the law indicates the need to remain vigilant regarding local health care availability, health insurance financial mechanics, small business law, tax code updating, and more. As information professionals, we have abundant work!

NOTES

1. See the full text of the Patient Protection and Affordable Care Act at https://www.govtrack.us/congress/bills/111/hr3590/text.

2. The federal government's Plain Language Initiative crosses all departments and offices. A website providing both explanations and toolkits is available at http://www.plainlanguage.gov.

3. Details about Medicaid coverage for adults eighteen to twenty-six who were previously in foster care can be found at http://www.medicaid.gov/State-Resource-Center/Downloads/Medicaid-and-CHIP-FAQs-Coverage-of-Former-Foster-Care-Children.pdf.

REFERENCES

American Library Association. 2008. "Code of Ethics of the American Library Association." http://www.ala.org/advocacy/proethics/codeofethics/codeethics.
Commonwealth of Massachusetts. 2006. 189th General Court, Chapter 58.
Fleming, Chris. 2010. "New *Health Affairs*: Acute but Nonemergency Patients Going to ERs." *Health Affairs Blog*, September 8. http://healthaffairs.org/blog/2010/09/08/new-health-affairs-acute-but-nonemergency-patients-going-to-ers/.
Henry J. Kaiser Family Foundation. 2012. "Explaining Healthcare Reform: Questions about Health Insurance Subsidies." July. https://kaiserfamilyfoundation.files.wordpress.com/2013/01/7962-02.pdf.

Chapter Two

Role of the Librarian

Margot Malachowski

In June 2013, the library community became entangled in the political fire-storm surrounding the Affordable Care Act (ACA). President Barack Obama called on librarians to become involved in a consumer education campaign on health care reform during the annual conference of the American Library Association (Young 2013). At that time, most of the news coverage focused on the process of selecting and purchasing affordable health insurance. Librarians were understandably confused as to their proper role in this endeavor. Librarians were accustomed to seeing themselves as advocates for early literacy, English as a second language, digital literacy, and even financial literacy. Many of them needed to think through how their role as literacy advocates would expand into health literacy and health insurance literacy. While health sciences librarians were particularly well positioned to make early connections between their work and the ACA, all librarians have the opportunity to leverage the ACA into new services for the populations that they serve.

The ACA is a lengthy and complex piece of legislation. The good news is that there are many entry points for library services. There are three main, identifiable roles for librarians: management of ACA information resources, instruction in the use of ACA information resources, and community building among ACA stakeholders. These roles go far beyond answering questions about health insurance enrollment. Librarians who step into these roles will be playing a part in improving the health of their communities. This chapter will provide explanations of each role and ideas for implementing these roles in many types of libraries.

HOSPITAL LIBRARIANS AND INFORMATION MANAGEMENT

President Obama signed the Affordable Care Act into law on March 23, 2010. Some of the first mandates were consumer protections such as prohibiting the denial of coverage based on preexisting conditions, eliminating lifetime limits on health insurance coverage, and the creation of an external review process for consumers appealing claim denials (Goldsmith outlines further details in chapter 1 of this book). Each year, additional health care reform mandates are launched (U.S. Department of Health and Human Services 2014b). Each phase of the ACA rollout creates new opportunities for librarians to manage ACA information resources.

For the hospital librarian, the implementation of electronic health records (EHRs) certified by the Office of the National Coordinator for Health Information Technology (ONC) brought health care reform into the workplace. This initiative predates the ACA but has important implications for patient engagement and cost containment. At the 2010 Medical Library Association Annual Meeting in Washington, DC, Charles P. Friedman, PhD, gave librarians a heads-up with an informative talk on the upcoming implementation of interoperable EHRs. At that time, Dr. Friedman was the chief scientific officer at the ONC in the U.S. Department of Health and Human Services. He explained that the Health Information Technology for Economic and Clinical Health (HITECH) Act was a part of the American Recovery and Reinvest-

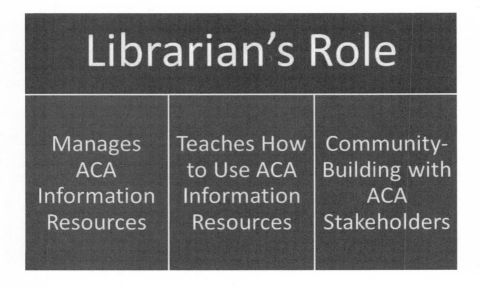

Figure 2.1.   The Librarian's Role in the Affordable Care Act.

ment Act of 2009. HITECH promotes the adoption and use of EHRs with a carrots-and-sticks approach. Through financial incentives and disincentives, HITECH encourages hospitals and physicians to make "meaningful use" of interoperable EHRs. Dr. Friedman described HITECH as a game changer, requiring not just the existence of technology but also improved health outcomes as a result of using the technology. He envisioned many opportunities for librarians. Quoting famed hockey player Wayne Gretzky, he encouraged us to "skate to where the puck is going to be" (Malachowski 2010).

Registration for the EHR incentive programs began in January 2011, with participating hospitals receiving incentive payments in May 2011 (Centers for Medicare and Medicaid Services 2014b). In March 2012, the ACA began requiring health plans to adopt and implement rules for the secure, confidential, and electronic exchange of health information (U.S. Department of Health and Human Services 2014b). Requirements for interoperable systems are a great match for hospital librarians with metadata skills. As stated by the President's Council of Advisors on Science and Technology in *Report to the President Realizing the Full Potential of Health Information Technology to Improve Healthcare of Americans: The Path Forward*, each unit of data in EHRs needs metadata describing its attributes, provenance, and required security protections (President's Council of Advisors on Science and Technology 2010). The initial requirements for interoperability are modest—sending prescriptions to a patient's preferred pharmacy—with a push to have medical records transferable within state borders. The Massachusetts Health Information Highway was one of the first to launch a statewide interoperable system. In October 2012, the health records of then-governor Deval Patrick were sent from Massachusetts General Hospital in Boston to Baystate Medical Center in Springfield (Modern Healthcare 2012). For librarians working closely with information technology departments, creating and managing metadata is a stellar opportunity to be involved in health care reform.

As early as 2007, some hospital librarians were exploring the potential for integrating library resources into EHRs. This grew out of the effort to transform hospital libraries from print repositories to managed, web-based information (Albert 2007). The result was that library resources were being utilized at the point of care in an unprecedented manner. Vendors were vying for a spot in EHRs. Librarians, accustomed to vendor negotiations, found themselves discussing new methods of information delivery. Incorporating library resources within EHRs is the first step to documenting electronically the use of evidence-based medicine in the treatment of disease. For example, printing personalized patient handouts, designed by vendors who are familiar to librarians, is the first step toward electronically documenting patient education. Documentation is an important part of proving the "meaningful use" of EHRs (Centers for Medicare and Medicaid Services 2014b). Librarians involved with selecting materials for EHRs will be contributing to this endeavor. In addition, this seamless integration of librarian-curated resources within EHRs will provide concrete evidence of how librarians contribute directly to patient care, providing an argument for the value of maintaining library services within the hospital and health care environment.

For the consumer health librarian, the transformation is just beginning. Upcoming mandates include promoting patient-generated health data (PGHD) as a decision support tool and launching patient portals to encourage consumer interaction. Research teams are experimenting with the best ways to capture, understand, interpret, and act upon PGHD, or the data provided by patients and family members (Deering 2013). Currently, much of this data is gathered at the point of care, but telemedicine and the use of mobile devices is changing the caregiving landscape. Data may be imported through apps and medical devices in the near future. Patient portals are likely to have a bumpy rollout, especially as consumers see incorrect or misleading information in their records. For hospital librarians working with patient education or marketing departments, this is a tremendous opportunity to get involved with patient engagement.

USING LIBGUIDES TO MANAGE ACA INFORMATION

Beyond participating in the nuts and bolts of EHRs, PGHD, and patient portals, hospital librarians are also creating LibGuides to manage information about the ACA. These guides are particularly useful in supporting hospital administrators and clinicians. For example, Alison Clapp at the Children's Hospital in Boston created a ready reference LibGuide for the hospital's leadership team (http://childrenshospital.libguides.com/content.php?pid=120656&sid=1454770). The "Health Care Reform" tab is a thorough resource, including links to journal articles, white papers, press releases, newspaper articles, policy reports, state laws, and the state-specific health insurance enrollment website.

For librarians in other settings, LibGuides may be the primary way of managing ACA information resources. Academic librarians are building subject guides to aid in the classroom study of the Affordable Care Act. Kevin Walker's LibGuide from the University of Alabama is a nice, clean example of an academic resource (http://guides.lib.ua.edu/ACA). His guide is customized for his academic audience and includes links to government and third-party websites, news articles, and academic databases. Walker includes a library catalog search box and his contact information for further assistance.

Documents librarian Sinai Wood created a Patient Protection and Affordable Care Act LibGuide for Baylor University (http://researchguides.baylor.edu/obamacare/). This guide puts the focus on the legislative aspects of the ACA. At Baylor, Wood specializes in government information, political science, and international studies. Her guide includes gentle instructions for employees looking for help with choosing their health insurance, clearly delineating the role of the librarian as information professional from the role of human resources as benefits advisors.

The ACA LibGuide from St. Louis Community College in is an excellent example of managing information resources at the community-college level (http://stlcc.v1.libguides.com/aca/). This guide, created by Rebecca Helbling, supports a specific sociology class—"SOC101: Affordable Care Act"—with key resources and a database search box.

LibGuides are used at the high school level as well. Marisa Anton, librarian at New Rochelle High School in New Rochelle, New York, created a guide on the Patient Protection and Affordable Care Act (http://nrhs.libguides.com/PPACA) in response to a class assignment on "Is President Obama's health care law unconstitutional?" Her guide supports the research requirements of the assignment with library resources and website links. She included a word search and audio and video files to enhance the learning experience.

Finally, public librarians are designing LibGuides to help consumers understand the ACA. Tulsa City-County Libraries in Tulsa, Oklahoma, has an effective guide (http://guides.tulsalibrary.org/ACA). Librarians Jessica Reed and Teresa Runnels developed this valuable resource for their community, including a listing of upcoming enrollment events, steps necessary in obtaining health insurance, and links to resources for small-business owners. The "Insurance Lingo" tab is particularly useful for consumers and includes a glossary of insurance terms from HealthCare.gov and the U.S. Department of Labor, as well as terms related to the Health Insurance Portability and Accountability Act (HIPAA).

National Network of Libraries of Medicine ACA Resources

- Greater Midwest Region (http://nnlm.gov/gmr/outreach/aca)
- Midcontinental Region (http://nnlm.gov/mcr/resources/aca.html)
- Middle Atlantic Region (http://nnlm.gov/mar/consumer/aca.html)
- New England Region (http://nnlm.gov/ner/training/aca.html)
- South Central Region (http://nnlm.gov/scr/outreach/aca.html)
- Southeastern/Atlantic Region (http://guides.nnlm.gov/sea/ACA)

The National Networks of Libraries of Medicine (NN/LM) are creating region-specific LibGuides on the Affordable Care Act (for specific links, please refer to the recommended resources outlined by Ham, Malloy, and Linares in chapter 7 of this book). Even within regions, each state has different regulations and resources. The NN/LM LibGuides (see sidebar) are a great starting point for any librarian interested in creating or updating ACA information resources for their institutions. For libraries that do not have LibGuide subscriptions, a dedicated web page serves the same function.

PROVIDING INSTRUCTION ON ACA RESOURCES

Instruction is the opportunity to leap off of the LibGuide and into a lively discussion. While managing information resources is a natural part of library work, instruction in the use of those resources is often overlooked. At a meeting of the Massachusetts Health Sciences Library Network meeting in 2014, Rebecca Blanchard, PhD, director of medical education and research at Baystate Medical Center in Springfield, Massachusetts, described approaching instruction like a ninja. Ninja instructors capture opportunistic teaching moments. These moments may or may not be identified as "instruction" by the learner or the librarian. This method differs from Samurai instruction, which is a more formal style with a classroom, lecture, and objectives (Blanchard 2014).

Hospital librarians do have formalized opportunities to present library resources, but often they have severe time limitations. For example, the onboarding of new medical residents might include a ten-minute introduction to the library. In such circumstances, hospital librarians use their time to showcase the best way to access library resources and to recommend several methods for contacting library staff. Hospital librarians may attend leadership meetings. At these meetings, they may receive a short allotment of time to give updates on the library. Most hospital library instruction occurs in flexible settings—during a department meeting, on a walk-in basis, or over the phone. The interaction may feel more like a reference interview, but instruction is taking place.

Demonstrating the use of LibGuides or library web pages is useful in a multitude of settings. Librarians providing instruction on ACA information resources will be working with adult learners. Adult learners, in particular, connect their prior experiences to the new subject matter. Adults will direct the librarian toward the information that they lack. A web-based resource, with designated boxes and tabs for various aspects of the Affordable Care Act, is useful for identifying the adult learner's specific information needs. For example, an administrator may zero in on the necessary policy report that she was looking for. A student may realize that he needs instruction in using a database. A consumer might take note of the steps required for obtaining health insurance, such as registering for an email address. LibGuides, or any visual aid, are extraordinarily helpful when trying to identify the learning need. For adult learners, this method quickly eliminates irrelevant material and focuses on the directly applicable information.

As the learner identifies the needed material, librarians will be able to point out additional resources available through the library. With ninja stealth, the librarian broadens the understanding of library services during the interaction. For example, a hospital administrator at Children's Hospital might not know that the Leadership LibGuide contains links for podcasts from *Harvard Business Review*. A clinician might not realize that there is a different LibGuide with video files of medical and surgical grand rounds. If the learner seems curious, a brief demonstration may open up another way for the librarian to support the learner. The key is to remain respectful of the learner's time and interests.

Academic librarians may have greater opportunities for delivering formalized instruction. As some of the highlighted LibGuides indicate, academic librarians are collecting resources specifically about the ACA. Some of these librarians may be integrated into classes, in true partnership with faculty. This integration increases the likelihood that students will seek further assistance from the librarian (Kesselman and Watstein 2009). A course may focus on the legal aspects of the ACA, requiring the librarian to provide instruction on the Federal Digital System (FDsys; available at http://www.gpo.gov/fdsys/). On the other hand, the focus may be on politics, creating an opportunity to teach how to use the Gale database Opposing Views in Context. Another course may be investigating preventive health measures and the impact of the ACA on community wellness programs. The librarian could guide students to the U.S. Department of Labor website for links to ACA-mandated research studies on preventive health care programs in the workplace (RAND Corporation 2013). The most effective LibGuide is well designed to align with the goals of faculty. Through instruction on relevant ACA resources, the librarian introduces valuable research strategies to students.

Increasingly, librarians are seeking out new measures for their instruction activities. "Connect, Collaborate, and Communicate: A Report from the Value of Academic Libraries Summits" recommends that librarians assess the impact of their instruction on the academic success of students. The hope is that this measure will bring greater attention to the value of librarians. Administrators, faculty, and professional staff are working together to provide a quality educational experience for students. Collaborative assessment will capture institutional effectiveness (Brown and Malenfant 2012). The same could be said in hospitals. The efforts of administrators, researchers, clinicians, and professional staff are combining to raise the quality of health care. Librarians assist hospital personnel by creating easy access to relevant information resources and by providing instruction in the use of those resources. Although ninja instruction is more challenging to document, those teaching outside of traditional academic contexts should investigate ways to articulate their contribution to the institutional understanding of the ACA.

TEACHING CONSUMERS ABOUT THE ACA

For librarians who work with consumers, the focus shifts toward health insurance enrollment procedures. Accustomed to helping consumers find all sorts of websites, librarians are now demonstrating where to find the health insurance marketplaces. Librarians are not encouraged to help consumers purchase insurance. Instead, federal and state governments provide trained navigators and certified application counselors to help the public with actual enrollment procedures. Michelle Eberle, health literacy and community engagement coordinator for the National Network of Libraries of Medicine, New England Region, identifies the librarian's role as an information professional and community resource (http://nnlm.gov/ner/training/aca.html). Librarians assist in health insurance enrollment by being familiar with ACA resources, including contact information for navigators and certified application counselors and by offering meeting space for public enrollment events (National Networks of Libraries of Medicine, New England Region 2014). This role is not distinctly different from the roles librarians take during tax season. Librarians demonstrate how to find tax forms, how to print forms, and may offer space to Volunteer Income Tax Assistance (VITA) volunteers. Librarians do not file taxes for the public.

Public librarians know that the consumers who ask for help with any website are often the people who need very basic computer assistance—logging on, printing documents, and opening email attachments. Some patrons are clearly overwhelmed by the digital world. This world of usernames, passwords, security questions, cookies, and caches is daunting for them. Most librarians are very cautious with helping consumers fill out forms of any sort. They will take a look to see why a patron is getting an error message after submitting. Even with a librarian's help, problems are not always resolved. Having referral information for navigators or certified application counselors is a huge relief to both the librarian and the consumer (Malachowski 2014).

Approximately one hundred library systems are publicly recognized as "Champions of Coverage" by the Centers for Medicare and Medicaid Services (Centers for Medicare and Medicaid Services 2014a). These libraries active provide information about the health insurance marketplace, participate in informational webinars, post Centers for Medicare and Medicaid Services (CMS) widgets and success stories, provide space for enrollment events, and connect with community partners. Librarians may join in the From Coverage to Care initiative sponsored by CMS. This initiative aims to help people new to health insurance. CMS provides print resources, online videos, and census data to help librarians identify and serve eligible uninsured populations. The key to reaching consumers is building relationships between the library and the surrounding community.

BUILDING COMMUNITY AMONG STAKEHOLDERS

President Obama's announcement at the American Library Association (ALA) conference ignited excitement over the presidential acknowledgment of the important role that librarians play in low-income neighborhoods (Young 2013). In many ways, libraries are resource centers for those most likely to be uninsured. Public libraries provide low-income neighborhoods with story times and summer reading programs, building foundations in early literacy. Librarians host classes in English as a second language and computer literacy. Low-income families have access to e-readers, and instruction in how to use these devices, through their public library. Librarians introduce the idea of financial literacy to their communities. Across the country, dozens of libraries have held Smart Investing @ Your Library events over the past decade (American Library Association 2015). Health literacy and health insurance literacy programming is based on the same principles. Librarians are offering opportunities for adults to gain the skills necessary for a productive and happy life.

Literacy programs depend on building community with fellow stakeholders. Many community organizations hold an interest in improving health outcomes for low-income populations. Hospitals and medical practices are directly impacted, but other organizations are concerned with health outcomes as well. Potential stakeholders include faith-based organizations; cul-

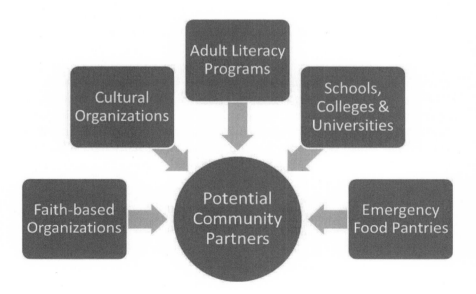

Figure 2.2. Potential Community Partners for Librarians.

tural organizations; adult literacy programs; schools, colleges, and universities; and emergency food pantries. Francisca Goldsmith, consultant and instructor at Infopeople, urges librarians to go beyond dropping off flyers at community organizations (Goldsmith 2015). Ask questions, develop relationships, and learn about the community through their eyes.

After President Obama's announcement in 2013, librarians prepared to help their communities. Across the nation, library staff participated in webinars to learn about new resources for the uninsured and underinsured. Three months later, the initial enrollment period held an unpleasant surprise—the HealthCare.gov website was unreliable. Librarians faced a paucity of questions rather than an overwhelming demand (Goldsmith 2015). For librarians who were eager to help, the failure of the website was a huge disappointment. "You never want a serious crisis to go to waste," advises Rahm Emanuel, former chief of staff for President Obama. "Crisis provides the opportunity for us to do things that you could not do before" (Seib 2008). Emanuel was describing a different crisis for the Obama administration, but the advice still applies. The failure of the HealthCare.gov website in 2013 did not deter librarians for preparing for the next enrollment year. The extra time allowed for the development of new ideas, additional training, and the time to identify fellow stakeholders.

Community building among stakeholders will yield benefits for years to come. By introducing health literacy and health insurance literacy programming to low-income communities, librarians will witness the struggle of those who lack information, or misunderstand information, about their health. Those struggles may be vast. In addition to witnessing great need, librarians report that they are concerned about pressure from their institutions to limit the amount of help they offer (Vardell 2014). These limits may be based on a perceived lack of library resources, in terms of both time and materials. Health and insurance information may be seen as outside the scope of library services. The most fundamental method of coping with the stress of limitations is to delineate the librarian's role as information professional from that of an insurance or health advisor. Librarians can then refer consumers to appropriate community resources, such as officially trained navigators. These referrals are simplified by established relationships with fellow stakeholders.

DOCUMENTING COMMUNITY BENEFITS

The ACA is lengthy and complex, with a timeline extending over many years. This legislation focuses on health promotion, disease prevention, information gathering, information dissemination, insurance reform, primary care expansion, and technology development (Hardcastle et al. 2011). Hospital librarians are aware of another aspect of the Affordable Care Act. ACA section 9007 alters the requirements for the charitable activities known as community benefits. Since 2010, the ACA requires that hospitals do the following:

- Conduct a community health needs assessment (CHNA) every three years
- Develop an implementation strategy based on needs identified in the CHNA
- Adopt and disseminate written policies on financial assistance and community care
- Limit charges, billing, and collections with respect to individuals eligible for financial assistance under the hospital's written policies

Hospitals have a long tradition of providing charity care to those who are unable to pay for services. In 1969, the Internal Revenue Service introduced IRS Form 990 for hospitals to document their charity work in exchange for federal tax exemptions. This work is referred to as "community benefits." IRS Schedule H was added in 2007, requiring additional details about community benefits. Hospitals may claim free and discounted health care, educational programs for health professionals, community improvement activities, as well as other activities designed to support the health of the neighborhoods they serve. The current ACA requirements add greater depth and transparency to the concept of community benefits (Nelson et al. 2013). These requirements provide an opportunity for hospital librarians to document their work.

For a hospital librarian, the first step is to identify what existing services count as community benefits. Librarians involved in continuing education that includes community health care providers or in research on community health that is to be published should count their time and resources as community benefits. Staff time at health fairs and community classes, the cost of materials freely distributed to community members, and community use of library space are countable as community benefits. The ACA pushes hospitals to track these types of activities and draw connections to the needs established by the CHNA. By reporting qualified activities to hospital administration, librarians are assisting their institutions in meeting the demands of the ACA.

Public and academic librarians have new opportunities as hospitals face changing reimbursement models in the coming years. The federal government is shifting away from the traditional Medicare and Medicaid fee-for-service structure. As part of this shift, future reimbursements will be linked to improved health outcomes for defined populations. The "population health" model is causing great concern for hospital administrators. Teaching hospitals, in particular, are anticipating drastic cuts in Medicare and Medicaid reimbursements (Keroack 2014). Hospitals are encouraged to explore payment models such as accountable care organizations (ACOs). ACOs are groups of doctors, hospitals, and other providers that coordinate care in order to reduce unnecessary spending. Care coordination and patient education are more important than ever. Additionally, the collaboration of community organizations, with a mutual goal of improving the health of low-income neighborhoods, will be critical to the success of population health (Morrissey 2012). Public and academic libraries are excellent community partners for any nonprofit hospital seeking to engage the public in promoting preventive health care and disease management.

Librarians have opportunities to create relevant services by managing ACA information resources, providing instruction in the use of ACA information resources, and building community among ACA stakeholders. Many librarians will take on the management of ACA information resources through involvement with EHRs, point-of-care tools, patient-generated health data, patient portals, LibGuides, and dedicated websites. Most librarians have an opportunity to instruct. In formal settings or with ninja stealth, librarians will introduce hospital administrators, faculty, clinicians, students, and consumers to valuable information about the ACA. Librarians are well positioned to build community. They will assist their own institutions by connecting people to appropriate resources. All librarians may take part in the enormous task of improving the health of their communities.

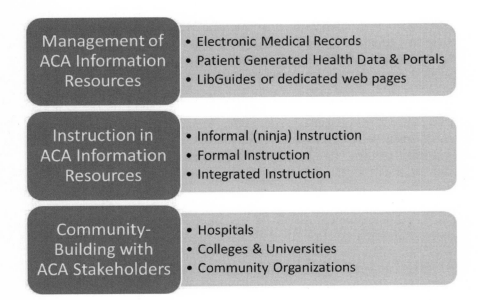

Figure 2.3.   Opportunities for Librarians.

For librarians interested in learning more, one of the best resources is OCLC's "Health Happens in Libraries" web page (http://www.webjunction.org/explore-topics/ehealth.html).

REFERENCES

Albert, Karen. 2007. "Integrating Knowledge-Based Resources into the Electronic Health Record." *Medical Reference Services Quarterly* 26(3):1–19.

American Library Association. 2015. "Smart Investing @ Your Library." http://smartinvesting.ala.org/.

Blanchard, Rebecca. 2014. "Ninja Teaching: Stealth Strategies to Conquer Any Teaching Scenario." Massachusetts Health Sciences Library Network meeting, Holyoke, Massachusetts, September 26.

Brown, Karen, and Kara J. Malenfant. 2012. "Connect, Collaborate and Communicate: A Report from the Value of Academic Libraries Summits." Association of College and Research Libraries.

Centers for Medicare and Medicaid Services. 2014a. "Champions for Coverage." September 17. https://marketplace.cms.gov/technical-assistance-resources/champions-for-coverage-list.pdf.

———. 2014b. "EHR Incentive Programs." http://www.cms.gov/Regulations-and-Guidance/Legislation/EHRIncentivePrograms/index.html.

Deering, Mary Jo. 2013. "Patient-Generated Health Data and Health IT." Issue Brief. Washington, DC: Office of the National Coordinator for Health Information Technology.

Goldsmith, Francisca. 2015. *Libraries and the Affordable Care Act.* Chicago: American Library Association.

Hardcastle, Lorian E., Katherine L. Record, Peter D. Jacobson, and Lawrence O. Gostin. 2011. "Improving the Population's Health: The Affordable Care Act and the Importance of Integration." Georgetown Public Law Research Paper, Georgetown University Law Center.

Keroack, Mark. 2014. "Baystate Health 2014 President's Report to the Organization." Annual Report. Springfield, MA: Baystate Health.

Kesselman, Martin A., and Sarah Barbara Watstein. 2009. "Creating Opportunities: Embedded Librarians." *Journal of Library Administration* 49(4):383–400.

Malachowski, Margot. 2010. "MLA 2010 Experience—Are You Experienced?" *Point Guard Librarian*, June 6. http://pointguardlibrarian.com/2010/06/.

———. 2014. "Obamacare and the Proper Role of Public Libraries in Health Literacy." *Computers in Libraries* 34(1):4–9.

Modern Healthcare. 2012. "Regional News/Northeast: Massachusetts Launches Statewide Health Info Exchange, and Other News." October 27. http://www.modernhealthcare.com/article/20121027/MAGAZINE/310279926.

Morrissey, John. 2012. "10 Facts about Population Health." *Trustee*, July 1, 10–14.

National Networks of Libraries of Medicine, New England Region. 2014. "The Affordable Care Act and Libraries." October 15. http://nnlm.gov/ner/training/aca.html.

Nelson, Gayle D., Martha H. Somerville, Carl H. Mueller, and Cynthia L. Boddie-Willis. 2013. "Hospital Community Benefits after the ACA." Issue Brief. Baltimore: Hilltop Institute.

President's Council of Advisors on Science and Technology. 2010. *Report to the President Realizing the Full Potential of Health Information Technology to Improve Healthcare for Americans: The Path Forward.* Executive Office of the President, December.

RAND Corporation. 2013. "Workplace Wellness Programs Study: Case Studies Summary Report." Office of Policy and Research, Employee Benefits Security Administration, Department of Labor, and Office of Health Policy, Assistant Secretary for Planning and Evaluation, Department of Health and Human Services. April.

Seib, Gerald. 2008. "In Crisis, Opportunity for Obama." *Wall Street Journal*, November 21. http://www.wsj.com/articles/SB122721278056345271.

U.S. Department of Health and Human Services. 2014a. "HHS Strategic Plan and Secretary's Strategic Initiatives." July 29. http://www.hhs.gov/strategic-plan/priorities.html.

———. 2014b. "Key Features of the Affordable Care Act by Year." http://www.hhs.gov/healthcare/facts/timeline/timeline-text.html.

Vardell, Emily. 2014. "Health Sciences Librarians' Response to Affordable Care Act Health Information Needs." October.

Young, Jeffery. 2013. "Obamacare Outreach Recruits Libraries." *Huffington Post*, July 1. http://www.huffingtonpost.com/2013/07/01/obamacare-libraries_n_3529849.html.

Chapter Three

Health Insurance Literacy

Implications for Librarian Involvement

Emily Vardell

This chapter presents an overview of health insurance literacy research. As information professionals providing a host of services, librarians must have some basic references and scholarly resources at our fingertips to serve as credible sources of information and guidance, particularly in discussions with professionals, funding sources, and decision makers. This chapter will provide an overview of the research and supporting sources for this purpose. It will also highlight evidence-based strategies for librarian involvement in health insurance and Affordable Care Act research and information services (summarized in the table near the end of this chapter).

SETTING THE STAGE FOR UNDERSTANDING HEALTH INSURANCE LITERACY

The American Medical Association developed one of the first formal definitions of health literacy in 1999, defining it as "the ability to read and comprehend prescription bottles, appointment slips, and the other essential health-related materials required to successfully function as a patient" (American Medical Association Council on Scientific Affairs, Ad Hoc Committee on Health Literacy 1999, 552). The definition has expanded over time, with Ratzan and Parker (2000) offering an oft-cited definition of health literacy as "the degree to which individuals have the capacity to obtain, process, and understand basic health information and services needed to make appropriate health decisions" (vi).

While health literacy and its ramifications on understanding general health information have been studied extensively, only a limited amount of research has been focused on health *insurance* literacy. In fact, though it may seem apparent that many individuals lack clear understanding of their health insurance, it is a "widely perceived but poorly documented problem" (Loewenstein et al. 2013, 851). One of the first formally proposed definitions of health insurance literacy describes it as "the extent to which consumers can make informed purchase and use decisions" (Kim, Braun, and Williams 2013, 3).

Employees have been making health insurance decisions for many years, and now the Affordable Care Act has brought the issue of health insurance literacy to the spotlight. Through the Affordable Care Act, millions of previously uninsured persons are making health insurance choices for the first time, and Americans with employer-sponsored insurance will see a change in coverage benefits (*Patient Protection and Affordable Care Act* 2010).

For the seventy-seven million adults with basic or below-basic health literacy (Kutner, Greenburg, Jin, and Paulsen 2006), the ability to procure appropriate levels of health insurance coverage and interact with the health care system successfully may be limited. Initial research in this area has shown that health insurance information materials are not written with low-literacy users in mind (Pati et al. 2012; Vardell 2013). To date, researchers have assessed health insurance literacy in selected populations (Cho, Lee, Arozullah, and Crittenden 2008; Hibbard, Jewett, Engelmann, and Tusler 1998; McCormack et al. 2009; Yin et al. 2009), as well as explored the effects of demographics (Hira and Loibl 2005; Sentell 2012) and human resources departments in health insurance education (Moses and Hogg 2009). To further the area of research in health insurance literacy levels, researchers at the American Institutes for Research have recently released a validated measure of health insurance literacy (Paez et al. 2014).

Because there have been limited studies on health insurance information seeking in libraries, this chapter casts a wider net for studies on health insurance literacy with a focus on the most salient conclusions for librarians. This chapter will discuss literacy concerns across the health insurance process, beginning with awareness of health insurance. Next, a model of health insurance literacy will be presented, followed by a discussion of large-scale assessments of health insurance literacy. A discussion of the role of choice in health insurance decision making; resistance to health insurance; and literacy demands in the health insurance process, with a focus on the readability of health insurance informational materials and forms, will follow. Finally, research on the role of human resources departments in addressing health insurance literacy will be explored.

AWARENESS OF HEALTH INSURANCE LITERACY

The first step in effective use of the health care system is awareness of the available resources. Federman et al. (2009) conducted a study of inner-city seniors to determine awareness of pharmaceutical cost-assistance programs. The researchers interviewed inner-city seniors about their awareness of programs, participation in health insurance presentations, and other demographic factors. Male gender, black race, inadequate health literacy (measured using the "Short Test of Functional Health Literacy in Adults"), and receiving care in a clinic setting (as opposed to private or group practice) were associated with low awareness of cost-assistance programs. Study participants who had heard a live presentation about health insurance were more likely to be aware of such programs. The authors suggest that their findings support the "use of live presentations, in addition to health literacy materials and messages, [as] . . . important strategies in promoting knowledge of and enrollment in state and federal pharmaceutical cost-assistance programs for low-income seniors" (127–29). Live presentations may be an effective tool for librarians seeking to improve patrons' health insurance literacy.

MODELS OF HEALTH INSURANCE LITERACY

McCormack et al.'s Conceptual Framework for Health Insurance Literacy

Using data collected from 1,202 Medicare beneficiaries, McCormack et al. (2009) developed a conceptual framework for health insurance literacy to "integrate a range of health- and insurance-related variables" (227). Their model includes factors such as health status, age, education, race, culture, financial literacy, numeracy (numeric literacy), health literacy, and health care decision making. Since these conclusions were drawn from a population of older adults, only 12.7 percent of whom were under age sixty-five, further studies should be conducted to extend the implications to a wider group.

The framework developed by McCormack et al. is novel in that it was the first to model health insurance literacy. In addition, it combines multiple facets, such as financial literacy and health literacy, building on strong areas of research ripe for further exploration in a new context.

Paez et al.'s Health Insurance Literacy Conceptual Model

In developing their Health Insurance Literacy Measurement (discussed further in the following section), Paez et al. (2014) created a health insurance literacy conceptual model. Their model identifies knowledge, information seeking, document literacy, and cognitive skills as the four domains that impact individuals' health insurance literacy, with self-efficacy as an under-lying domain. These domains were identified through a combination of a literature review, key informant interviews, and a stakeholder group. They are operationalized in Paez et al.'s Health Insurance Literacy Measurement (see next section, "Assessments of Health Literacy and Health Insurance Literacy").

In comparing the two models/frameworks for health insurance literacy, the model presented by Paez et al. includes more domain-specific tasks, such as completing health insurance forms, calculating cost sharing, and other insurance-related skills to model the concept. McCormack et al. focus more on the underlying causes of differences in health insurance literacy, such as demographics and health status. Barnes, Hanoch, and Rice (2015) stress the multidimensionality of this topic, stating that health insurance literacy is "likely influenced by cognitive abilities consumers possess (e.g., numeracy) and the amount of information available in the decision environment" (60). It may be necessary to combine multiple models to create a fuller picture of health insurance literacy, understanding both the individual characteristics as well as individual abilities that form an individual's health insurance literacy.

ASSESSMENTS OF HEALTH LITERACY AND HEALTH INSURANCE LITERACY

More than one quarter of the population with employer-based insurance dem-onstrated little to no "simple and concrete literacy skills" (Kutner, Green-burg, Jin, and Paulsen 2006, 5) in the 2003 National Assessment of Adult Literacy (NAAL). The U.S. Department of Education National Center for Education Statistics administered the NAAL to more than nineteen thousand adults, making the NAAL the largest-scale measurement of health literacy in the United States to date. A total of 24 percent of the adult participants with employer-based insurance had basic or below-basic health literacy skills (17 percent had basic health literacy and 7 percent had below-basic health litera-cy).

While the greatest percentage of adults with employer, military, or private insurance had intermediate or proficient health literacy, individuals with Medicare, Medicaid, or no insurance had the greatest percentage of below-basic health literacy (more than half of that population had basic or below-basic health literacy skills; 25 percent had basic health literacy and 28 per-cent had below-basic literacy). This statistic is particularly important for those offering ACA-related outreach, as individuals with no insurance com-prise the majority of those seeking insurance within the health insurance marketplace. In addition, individuals who struggle the most with understand-ing health care information were more likely to be sixty-five or older, male, black or Hispanic, or have spoken another language besides English prior to formal education. These findings are a strong reminder that health literacy skills cannot be generalized to particular populations. While there are demonstrable trends, low health literacy levels can be observed in portions of most populations and should be taken into consideration when librarians offer one-on-one health insurance assistance or support.

The Health Insurance Literacy Measurement (HILM) Project at the American Institutes for Research released a measurement of health insurance literacy in October 2014 (Paez et al. 2014). The HILM comprises four scales. The first two are designed to understand how individuals select a health plan by asking individuals to report their confidence in choosing a health plan and their behavior regarding comparing health insurance plans. The second two scales assess how consumers navigate and use health plans by asking individuals to report their confidence and past behavior with using health insurance. The HILM is available to those who register for an account at http:// healthinsliteracy.airprojects.org/. Because the measurement has only recently been publicly available, there are not yet any other published studies that employ the HILM. Those interested in conducting studies of patrons and their health insurance literacy skills may want to use this measurement to obtain baseline data of participants' abilities.

CHOICE AND HEALTH INSURANCE

Once patients are aware of their health care plan options, they are confronted with a barrage of insurance choices. Hibbard, Jewett, Engelmann, and Tusler (1998) conducted a study of 1,673 Medicare beneficiaries to assess ability to make informed choices about fee-for-service (FFS) and managed care options. Their cross-sectional telephone survey results indicated that participants use a variety of information sources to learn about health plans, with an average of 2.8 sources each. For both health maintenance organization (HMO) and traditional Medicare enrollees, HMO advertisements were the most common information source for learning about health plans. In addition, "30 percent of beneficiaries know almost nothing about HMOs; only 11 percent have adequate knowledge to make an informed choice; and HMO enrollees have significantly lower knowledge levels of the differences between the two delivery systems" (181).

These findings have implications for educating beneficiaries about their expanded choices and highlight the importance of addressing information needs in this population, as well as their susceptibility to "aggressive marketing." Hibbard, Jewett, Engelmann, and Tusler encourage moving from mere information dissemination to active education. Targeted educational efforts aimed at intermediaries such as patient advocates, consumer health librarians, family members, and health professionals will be needed to enhance their ability to assist seniors in making informed health care choices.

McCormack et al. (2009) used principles of financial literacy, coupled with previous research on health literacy, to examine health insurance literacy. Their group created a two-part instrument to assess health insurance literacy, including questions designed to gauge prior knowledge and familiarity with health insurance terminology and questions aimed at assessing proficiency using the Medicare insurance system (as their focus was on older adults). The study sample was made up of 1,202 Medicare beneficiaries participating in the longitudinal Medicare Current Beneficiary Survey. For the terminology section, the terms that were the most misunderstood included "provider network" (41 percent), "formulary" (44 percent), and "Medigap" (56 percent). This indicates a lack of prior knowledge of insurance concepts and supports the need for dictionaries or glossaries in Medicare informational materials, such as the handbook *Medicare & You*. These tools should be linked from library information portals or included in library collections as appropriate.

In the proficiency exercises designed by McCormack et al. (2009), the questions requiring interpretation of the Medicare Explanation of Benefits form proved to be the most difficult. The authors demonstrated that "certain vulnerable subgroups also had significantly lower levels of health insurance literacy relative to their counterparts" (236), including adults over the age of eighty-five, women, ethnic minorities, adults from a lower socioeconomic level, and those who reported a lower health status. A 2005 systematic review of health literacy research corroborates these findings as it demonstrated that lower levels of health literacy are associated with level of education, ethnicity, and age; however, the systematic review also demonstrated that lower health literacy is not associated with gender or measurement instrument (Paasche-Orlow et al. 2005). The relationship between gender and health insurance literacy may require additional research due to conflicting findings, some of which show males with lower health insurance literacy (Federman et al. 2009; Kutner, Greenburg, Jin, and Paulsen 2006), while others show women with lower levels (McCormack et al. 2009).

In summary, while health literacy is defined by experts as "the degree to which individuals have the capacity to obtain, process, and understand basic health information" (Ratzan and Parker 2000, vi), health care consumers may face other barriers in making health insurance choices. Studies have shown that lack of familiarity with common terms can often impact patient's interactions with insurance materials (McCormack et al. 2009). In addition, aspects of financial literacy often impact the decision-making process (Hira and Loibl 2005; Moses and Hogg 2009). Finally, those with poorer health insurance literacy have been shown to have poorer health status and health outcomes (McCormack et al. 2009; Cho, Lee, Arozullah, and Crittenden 2008; Sentell 2012).

LITERACY DEMANDS IN THE HEALTH INSURANCE PROCESS

Each year the 150 million Americans with employer-sponsored health insurance (Kaiser Family Foundation 2014) must select their preferred insurance coverage option from a handful of choices. These decisions are often made with only summary of benefits and coverage (SBC) forms as guides. SBC forms are designed to provide standardized information about different options to enable employees to select their optimal option. Assessments of health insurance informational materials have demonstrated high literacy demands (Pati et al. 2012; Vardell 2013), indicating that individuals with lower health literacy levels may not have the skills necessary to interpret SBC forms.

There is a growing trend in health care to encourage healthy individuals to enroll in consumer-directed health plans. Consumer-directed health plans (CDHPs), or low co-pay, high deductible plans, require enrollees to compare costs between providers and treatment options. Those who do not have high levels of health insurance literacy may not have the skills to participate effectively in a consumer-directed health plan. The disconnect between insurance plan literacy demands and the literacy levels of enrollees may increase health disparities and health care costs among a large portion of the population (Miller 2007).

Greene, Peters, Mertz, and Hibbard (2008) explored the literacy demands of consumer-directed health plans by devising six different formats for displaying health plan information. They demonstrated that side-by-side comparisons were more effective at conveying CDHP information than pulling out common or unique information for CDHPs. In their test of a framework designed to summarize CDHPs advantages and disadvantages, results showed that a framework actually reduced comprehension for those who are less numerate. Conversely, the frameworks increased comprehension for those with higher levels of numeracy; however, both groups (i.e., both those with high and low numeracy) reported that the frameworks were difficult to understand. In addition, the results indicated that the numeracy level of participants was the greatest indicator of comprehension, above literacy, presentation of information, and socio-demographic factors. These findings have implications for the push for higher enrollment in CDHPs, as well as other health care plans, including those selecting from the available options in the health insurance marketplace.

The literacy demands on Medicaid consumers were explored in a study by Greene and Peters (2009). This study grew out of a project from Florida's

Medicaid Program, which adopted value-driven health care initiatives, requiring similar demands as CDHPs. In focus groups of Medicaid consumers,
Greene and Peters determined that while participants were enthusiastic about
having choices in their health care coverage, this "enthusiasm did not trans-
late into comparison shopping for health plans" (25).

The findings from Greene and Peters (2009) and Green, Peters, Mertz,
and Hibbard (2008) suggest that presentation approaches may need to be
customized to the numeracy levels of the audience. Their results confirmed
the hypothesis that simplified presentation strategies (e.g., lowering the reading level of the presented information and creating a less complex chart of
information) would increase information comprehension. Steps that librarians can take to decrease the complexity of shared information include in-
creasing font size, ordering information in a germane way (e.g., in order of
cost), and simplifying layout (e.g., reducing the number of columns).

Lawson, Carreón, Veselovskiy, and Escarce (2011) explored the role of
culturally and linguistically appropriate services in health insurance literacy.
They surveyed 123 health plans about their language data collection and
determined that 74 percent of health plans collected language data (commer-
cial 60.0 percent, Medicaid 89.1 percent, Medicare 91.7 percent). Nearly all
of the health plans reported offering language services, including interpretation services via phone, multilingual informational handouts, and access to
bilingual providers. The authors suggested that the "availability of a full
range of culturally and linguistically appropriate health care services is essential for overcoming barriers and accessing timely care" (e479).

READABILITY OF HEALTH INSURANCE MATERIALS

Yin et al. (2009) extracted data from the 2003 NAAL to explore the ability to
fill out health insurance forms by the parents of young children. In this
population of 6,100 parents, 68.4 percent were unable to properly complete a
health insurance form, and 65.9 percent were unable to calculate the annual
cost of a health insurance policy on the basis of family size. Perhaps it
follows logically that the parents with below-basic health literacy were more
likely to have a child without health insurance in their household. The authors conclude that given the large proportion of U.S. parents with low health
literacy, "decreasing literacy demands on parents, including simplification of
health insurance and other medical forms . . . is needed to decrease healthcare
access barriers for children and . . . ameliorate existing child health disparities" (S289).

The reading levels of Medicaid and other health care plan applications
continue to be a popular research area. Pati et al. (2012) examined compli-
ance of Medicaid-renewal applications to the established state reading level

guidelines. The reading levels were assessed using three readability tests: Flesch-Kincaid Grade Level Index, New Fog Count, and FORCAST. As of 2008, forty-five states had reading level guidelines for the Medicaid-related materials, yet twenty-four (52.2 percent) of the states failed to meet their guidelines on all three readability tests. As the authors emphasize, "complying with established reading level guidelines for Medicaid-related materials is one simplification strategy that should be implemented to improve access" (297).

Wallace, DeVoe, and Hansen (2011) conducted a more holistic assessment of Children's Health Insurance Program (CHIP) applications by assessing reading demands, layout characteristics, and document complexity. They assessed these characteristics of online English-language (n = 50) and Spanish-language (n = 39) Medicaid/CHIP enrollment applications through Lexile Analyzer (to assess reading demands), the User-Friendliness Tool (to assess layout), and the PMOSE/IKIRSCH scale (to assess document complexity). While the low-literacy guidelines state that applications should be written at a sixth grade or lower reading level and using a font of twelve points or larger, the results showed that the application "Signature" pages were written at a high school reading level and only five enrollment applications (5.6 percent) consistently used a twelve-point or larger font size throughout. Wallace, DeVoe, and Hansen determined that document complexity was above recommended levels, with the majority of the applications ranking at level 4 (high). In addition, the authors noted that to increase access for all populations, every state should provide an online Spanish-language version of the Medicaid/CHIP enrollment application, whereas at the time of their study only thirty-nine of the states provided a Spanish-language version.

To address these demonstrated gaps, Gazmararian, Beditz, Pisano, and Carreón (2010), comprising a team of researchers from Emory University and America's Health Insurance Plans, sought to develop a health literacy assessment tool for health plans. They designed the tool to serve as a benchmark to address the "magnitude and consequences of low health literacy . . . [and] the role health plans are playing and the activities they undertake to address this problem" (93). The areas of focus were identified through discussion with health plan representatives and a brief survey of health plans. Through this work researchers proposed six main areas of evaluation: information for members/navigation, member services/communication, web navigation, forms, nurse call line, and nurse case/disease management. They conducted a pilot study of their assessment tool on eight health plans. After incorporating reactions from this pilot study, the researchers launched the full assessment tool in 2009, and it is available at https://www.ahip.org/HealthLiteracy/.

The Maine Area Health Education Center (AHEC) Health Literacy Center created a national skills training workshop called "Writing for the Medicaid Market" to address the issue of a lack of easy-to-read Medicaid materials (Root and Stableford 1999). The Maine AHEC Health Literacy Center designed the training for public and private organizations providing Medicaid managed care services, gearing the training toward alleviating the mismatch between the low literacy skills of the target population and the high reading level of most health and managed care materials. While post-training survey data demonstrated that the workshop was successful, the authors state that "faulty and/or nonexistent communication planning limits the success" (1). That is, lack of attention to relaying the changes in Medicaid to consumers has effectively resulted in widespread confusion. Workshops and assessment tools that promote the skills necessary to develop easy-to-read application materials provide a starting off point for greater discussion of building effective health insurance systems.

RESISTANCE TO HEALTH INSURANCE

Villaire and Mayer (2009) contend that if patients are empowered to use health care services more effectively by funding preventive and education measures, "we end up with a true health care system, rather than a sick care system" (56). In addition, there is a better chance of achieving positive health outcomes and a reduction of necessary use of the health care system, with a final outcome of a "system that costs a lot less" (56). However, prior to the Affordable Care Act, many Americans elected not to obtain health insurance (the individual mandate now requires all Americans to obtain health insurance). In an effort to determine reasons for resistance to health insurance, researchers used theories of behavioral economics and polling data to study those who elected not to obtain health insurance. Their findings may also have implications for resistance to the Affordable Care Act and other barriers to enrollment.

Baicker, Congdon, and Mullainathan (2012) used the theories of behavioral economics, a combination of psychology and economic analysis, to explore why uninsured Americans do not take advantage of the insurance options available to them. They point out that "while prices and information are undeniably key factors for understanding and achieving socially optimal health insurance coverage, . . . there is mounting evidence that a third factor, the psychology of individual decision making, plays a central role in driving coverage outcomes" (108–9).

Baicker, Congdon, and Mullainathan demonstrated that transaction costs such as long Medicaid applications and social stigma can impede enrollment. Assistance with enrollment has been proven to increase participation, presenting a strong argument for librarians to offer support in this area. An additional reason for nonenrollment may be the perception of limited bene-

Table 3.1. Evidence-Based Strategies for Addressing Health Insurance Literacy Needs

Article	Evidence-Based Strategy
Baicker, Congdon, and Mullainathan (2012)	Assistance with enrollment has been proven to increase participation, presenting a strong argument for librarians to offer support in this area.
Federman et al. (2009)	Live presentations may be an effective tool for librarians seeking to improve patrons' health insurance literacy.
Greene, Peters, Mertz, and Hibbard (2008)	Steps that librarians can take to decrease the complexity of shared information include increasing font size, ordering information in a germane way (e.g., in order of cost), and simplifying layout (e.g., reducing the number of columns).
Hibbard, Jewett, Engelmann, and Tusler (1998)	Targeted educational efforts aimed at intermediaries such as patient advocates, consumer health librarians, family members, and health professionals will be needed to enhance their ability to assist seniors in making informed healthcare choices.
Kutner, Greenburg, Jin, and Paulsen (2006)	Low health literacy levels can be observed in portions of most populations and should be taken into consideration when librarians offer one-on-one health insurance assistance or support.
McCormack et al. (2009)	Dictionaries or glossaries in Medicare and other insurance informational materials, such as the handbook *Medicare & You*, should be linked from library information portals or included in library collections as appropriate.
Paez et al. (2014)	Those interested in conducting studies of patrons and their health insurance literacy skills may want to use the Health Insurance Literacy Measurement (HILM) to obtain baseline data of participants' abilities.
Root and Stableford (1999)	Workshops and assessment tools that promote the skills necessary to develop easy-to-read application materials provide a starting off point for greater discussion of building effective health insurance systems.

fits, as the true benefit only arises once one is sick and requires medical attention. Individuals can actually make better-informed choices through their employers, particularly when employers provide a short list of options for employees to choose from, as well as provide administrators to offer guidance.

CONCLUSION

Barnes, Hanoch, and Rice (2015) drive home the importance of providing assistance with health insurance literacy concerns: "whether the policy goals for the Affordable Care Act are achieved will be shaped in no small part by the extent of Americans becoming engaged consumers of health insurance. To do so . . . they will need a great deal of help understanding and comparing coverage options when making these important decisions" (76). While health literacy is certainly a key aspect of health insurance literacy, health care consumers may face additional barriers in understanding health insurance information. Studies have shown that a lack of familiarity with common terms can often impact patients' interactions with insurance materials (McCormack et al. 2009). In addition, aspects of financial literacy often impact the decision-making process (Hira and Loibl 2005; Moses and Hogg 2009).

The evidence-based strategies suggested throughout this chapter are summarized in table 3.1. Librarians can play a role in supporting health insurance information needs by locating and advocating for easy-to-understand information, linking to helpful insurance resources (e.g., healthcare.gov or *Medicare & You*), and offering live presentations of pertinent health insurance information (for further discussion of librarians' roles, please refer to chapter 2 of this book). The concrete and practical suggestions offered by the evidence presented in this chapter demonstrate the relevance of librarians to health insurance literacy research and interventions.

REFERENCES

American Medical Association, Council on Scientific Affairs, Ad Hoc Committee on Health Literacy. 1999. "Health Literacy: Report of the Council on Scientific Affairs." *Journal of the American Medical Association* 281(6):552–57.

Baicker, K., W. J. Congdon, and S. Mullainathan. 2012. "Health Insurance Coverage and Take-Up: Lessons from Behavioral Economics." *Milbank Quarterly* 90(1):107–34.

Barnes, A. J., Y. Hanoch, and T. Rice. 2015. "Determinants of Coverage Decisions in Health Insurance Marketplaces: Consumers' Decision-Making Abilities and the Amount of Information in Their Choice Environment." *Health Services Research* 50(1):58–80.

Cho, Y. I., S. Y. D. Lee, A. M. Arozullah, and K. S. Crittenden. 2008. "Effects of Health Literacy on Health Status and Health Service Utilization amongst the Elderly." *Social Science & Medicine (1982)* 66(8):1809–16.

Federman, A. D., D. G. Safran, S. Keyhani, H. Cole, E. A. Halm, and A. L. Siu. 2009. "Awareness of Pharmaceutical Cost-Assistance Programs among Inner-City Seniors." *American Journal of Geriatric Pharmacotherapy* 7(2):117–29.

Gazmararian, J. A., K. Beditz, S. Pisano, and R. Carreón. 2010. "The Development of a Health Literacy Assessment Tool for Health Plans." *Journal of Health Communication* 15 (Suppl. 2): 93–101.

Greene, J., and E. Peters. 2009. "Medicaid Consumers and Informed Decisionmaking." *Health Care Financing Review* 30(3):25–40.

Greene, J., E. Peters, C. K. Mertz, and J. H. Hibbard. 2008. "Comprehension and Choice of a Consumer-Directed Health Plan: An Experimental Study." *American Journal of Managed Care* 14(6):359–76.

Hibbard, J. H., J. J. Jewett, S. Engelmann, and M. Tusler. 1998. "Can Medicare Beneficiaries Make Informed Choices?" *Health Affairs* 17(6):181–93.

Hira, T. K., and C. Loibl. 2005. "A Gender Perspective on the Use of Supplemental Healthcare Plans." *International Journal of Consumer Studies* 29(4):319–31.

Kaiser Family Foundation. 2014. "Health Insurance Coverage of the Total Population." http://kff.org/other/state-indicator/total-population/.

Kim, J., B. Braun, and A. D. Williams. 2013. "Understanding Health Insurance Literacy: A Literature Review." *Family and Consumer Sciences Research Journal* 42(1):3–13.

Kutner, M., E. Greenburg, Y. Jin, and C. Paulsen. 2006. *The Health Literacy of America's Adults: Results from the 2003 National Assessment of Adult Literacy.* NCES 2006-483. Washington, DC: National Center for Education Statistics.

Lawson, E. H., R. Carreón, G. Veselovskiy, and J. J. Escarce. 2011. "Collection of Language Data and Services Provided by Health Plans." *American Journal of Managed Care* 17(12):e479–87.

Loewenstein, G., J. Y. Friedman, B. McGill, et al. 2013. "Consumers' Misunderstanding of Health Insurance." *Journal of Health Economics* 32(5):850–62.

McCormack, L., C. Bann, J. Uhrig, N. Berkman, and R. Rudd. 2009. "Health Insurance Literacy of Older Adults." *Journal of Consumer Affairs* 43(2):223–48.

Miller, V. M. 2007. "Poor eHealth Literacy and Consumer-Directed Health Plans: A Recipe for Market Failure." *American Journal of Bioethics* 7(11):20–22.

Moses, J., and B. Hogg. 2009. "Benefits Literacy, Bugs Bunny and Bridge." *Benefits Quarterly* 25(3):20–27.

Paasche-Orlow, M. K., R. M. Parker, J. A. Gazmararian, L. T. Nielsen-Bohlman, and R. Rudd. 2005. "The Prevalence of Limited Health Literacy." *Journal of General Internal Medicine* 20(2):175–84.

Paez, K. A., C. J. Mallery, H. Noel, C. Pugliese, V. E. McSorely, J. L. Lucado, and D. Ganachari. 2014. "Development of the Health Insurance Literacy Measure (HILM): Conceptualizing and Measuring Consumer Ability to Choose and Use Private Health Insurance." *Journal of Health Communication* 19 (Suppl. 2): 225–39.

Pati, S., J. E. Kavanagh, S. K. Bhatt, A. T. Wong, K. Noonan, and A. Cnaan. 2012. "Reading Level of Medicaid Renewal Applications." *Academic Pediatrics* 12(4):297–301.

Patient Protection and Affordable Care Act. 2010. Public Law 148, 111th Cong., 2nd sess.

Ratzan, S. C., and R. M. Parker. 2000. "Introduction." In *National Library of Medicine Current Bibliographies in Medicine: Health Literacy,* edited by C. R. Selden, M. Zovn, S. C. Ratzan, and R. M. Parker. NLM Pub N. CBM 2000-1. Bethesda, MD: National Institutes of Health, U.S. Department of Health and Human Services.

Root, J., and S. Stableford. 1999. "Easy-to-Read Consumer Communications: A Missing Link in Medicaid Managed Care." *Journal of Health Politics, Policy and Law* 24(1):1–26.

Sentell, T. 2012. "Implications for Reform: Survey of California Adults Suggests Low Health Literacy Predicts Likelihood of Being Uninsured." *Health Affairs (Project Hope)* 31(5):1039–48.

Vardell, E. 2013. "Readability Levels of Health Insurance Summary of Benefits and Coverage Forms." Paper presented at the annual conference of the Medical Library Association, Boston, May.

Villaire, M., and G. Mayer. 2009. "Health Literacy: The Low-Hanging Fruit in Health Care Reform." *Journal of Health Care Finance* 36(2):55–59.

Wallace, L. S., J. E. DeVoe, and J. S. Hansen. 2011. "Assessment of Children's Public Health Insurance Program Enrollment Applications: A Health Literacy Perspective." *Journal of Pediatric Health Care* 25(2):133–37.

Yin, H. S., M. Johnson, A. L. Mendelsohn, M. A. Abrams, L. M. Sanders, and B. P. Dreyer. 2009. "The Health Literacy of Parents in the United States: A Nationally Representative Study." *Pediatrics* 124 (Suppl. 3): S289–98.

Chapter Four

The Health Insurance Reference Question

A Step-by-Step Approach

Deborah H. Charbonneau and Kelli Ham

The implementation of the Affordable Care Act (ACA) presents a number of opportunities for librarians to support the health insurance information needs of their communities. Public libraries have a tradition of providing consumer health information (Murray 2008). Moreover, public libraries are known to offer access to computers and free Internet service, thereby helping to bridge the digital divide in many communities by offering technical assistance for accessing information (Linnan et al. 2004).

The ACA may prompt questions about health benefits, health insurance marketplace deadlines, or state health exchanges. Harris et al. (2010) wonder where citizens "will acquire information and adequate resources" if they are unable to find relevant answers to questions about their health from the health care system (251). American Library Association President Barbara Stripling states, "research shows that Americans regularly turn to their local libraries as a trusted resource for information regarding government initiatives and programs" (American Library Association 2013). As such, libraries are uniquely situated to also play a critical role in helping consumers navigate the health insurance landscape.

The aim of this chapter is to provide a step-by-step approach for responding to health insurance reference questions. In this chapter, the term "reference work" is used broadly to refer to in-person, telephone, and electronic reference transactions. The Consumer and Patient Health Information Section (CAPHIS) of the Medical Library Association (MLA) states that librarians engage in activities "oriented towards the social and community goals of producing a healthy society as well as assisting the individual to make more informed health decisions" (CAPHIS 1996). Overall, librarians can play an important role in facilitating access to quality and unbiased health insurance information.

CONSUMER HEALTH REFERENCE IN LIBRARIES

Harris et al. (2010) note the emerging "healthwork" roles in public libraries. In particular, public libraries can provide "an important starting place to fill information gaps about health concerns" (250). As libraries continue to play a vital role in providing health and health-related insurance information, a number of professional sources can guide health reference interviews.

An essential component of providing relevant reference services is knowing about the community served. Library communities are really composites of many smaller "microcosms affiliated by culture, language, economic status, family structure, and other demographic and affinity characteristics" (Goldsmith 2015, 21). Demographics of the community will identify the characteristics of the target audience, including populations, ethnic backgrounds, socioeconomic statuses, education levels, and languages spoken. All of these elements provide clues that help librarians develop appropriate resources and services. Taking this concept to a more focused level, knowing the health status and health information needs of the community are essential for providing quality reference service for health insurance and health information.

For example, it may come as a surprise that the ACA includes a provision that requires nonprofit hospitals to publish detailed community health needs assessments (CHNAs) every three years. These publicly available reports provide a treasure trove of information about community health and can be found with an Internet search for a city, county, or hospital name combined with the phrase "community health needs assessment." Each report will provide demographic breakdowns and identify the most pressing health needs of the community, including prevalence of underinsured or lack of insurance coverage in the population. Librarians can take advantage of the work already done; once the health status and needs of the community are known, the library can assess services and plan for improvements as needed. Using community health needs reports and information will help librarians provide tailored health insurance information for library users.

The National Network of Libraries of Medicine (NN/LM) highlights a number of important considerations for librarians related to the provision of consumer health information. Topics ranging from issues and barriers to best practices and strategies for successful interactions are addressed in "Consumer Health Reference Interview & Ethical Issues" (NN/LM 2015). Key rec-

ommendations gleaned from the NN/LM guidelines provide a useful framework for providing health insurance reference. The guidelines that follow
have been adapted and supplemented with additional recommendations to
reflect the growing involvement of librarians in providing health insurance
information to library users.

GENERAL GUIDELINES FOR HEALTH INSURANCE REFERENCE

1. **Provide a welcoming, safe environment.** As health issues may be
   personal and sensitive, a number of things can be done to help create a
   welcoming environment. This advice applies to the provision of health
   insurance information as well. For in-person reference interactions,
   "welcoming behaviors [include] making eye contact, smiling, and
   greeting the patron" (NN/LM 2015). Fostering a welcoming, safe environment can be extended to the telephone and virtual environment.
   A friendly, helpful voice on the phone or an online "welcome message" can invite library patrons, create a welcoming presence during
   reference transactions, and set the overall tone for reference communication. Patrons may need to provide private information in order to
   receive a thorough, accurate answer, so assurances to patrons about
   confidentiality during insurance-related reference transactions can further contribute to building trust and creating a "safe" environment.
   Such confidentiality notices can be included in email communications
   and displayed during chat reference services. Be alert for signs that the
   patron is uncomfortable when others might overhear the conversation;
   move to more private places when possible for discussing sensitive
   health or insurance topics. Ensuring patron privacy is essential; libraries can install privacy screens on computer monitors for visual privacy, and computers can include secure software that resets the browser
   history at the end of each session. These measures will provide the
   necessary levels of confidentiality and security for patrons.
2. **Be aware of the individual asking the question.** Individuals may
   seek health insurance information for themselves. However, other
   family members, friends, or caregivers may be inquiring about health
   insurance options on behalf of someone else. Therefore, it is important
   to determine the context of the health insurance reference question,
   including the role of the person asking the question. Age range, special circumstances, and geographic location might be factors to consider as well with regard to health insurance options. The U.S. Department of Health and Human Services provides an online resource with
   an interactive map of the United States for state-by-state information
   (http://www.hhs.gov/healthcare/facts/bystate/statebystate.html).   An-

other helpful resource is healthinsurance.org, which furnishes information on affordable health and medical coverage for all states. In
addition, benefits from health programs, such as Medicaid, Medicare,
and the Children's Health Insurance Program (CHIP), may vary depending on age (e.g., older adults).

3. **Get as much information as possible using open-ended questions.**
An important step of the reference interview is to "use open-ended,
neutral questions to find as much information as possible about what
the person wants to know" (NN/LM 2015). Questions that are phrased
neutrally and are open-ended are more efficient and can help guide the
process. For example, "Can you tell me how you will use this information?" will prompt essential information, whereas closed questions,
such as "Will you use this information to help enroll in a plan?"
require more follow-up questions and can inadvertently expose as-
sumptions. When helping patrons to understand health insurance options or navigate the process of signing up for health coverage, it can
be helpful to ask what sources of information have already been con-
sulted and how far along they are in the process. In this way, librarians
can decipher what is already known, which sources of information
have been useful (or not useful), and then direct patrons accordingly to
other relevant health insurance sources and tools.

4. **Verify terminology in a dictionary or encyclopedia.** An individual
"might not know the correct medical terminology to describe his or
her health condition" (NN/LM 2015). As a result, verifying terminology in a medical dictionary or encyclopedia is a common consumer
health reference practice. In the ACA landscape, individuals and librarians alike may not be familiar with a range of health insurance
terminology, health care laws, or legal terms. Online glossaries and
dictionaries can be very helpful in this regard to verify health insurance terms. For example, the Healthcare.gov site provides a freely
accessible online glossary (https://www.healthcare.gov/glossary/). Individual state exchange websites will often include a glossary with
terms that are specific to that state.

5. **Recognize the limitations of information formats.** Library users
may have expectations about the information available for health insurance. Patrons may desire information in a variety of formats that
clearly explains their health plan options in order to make informed
decisions. The nature of the ACA and enrolling in plans has put the
spotlight on the digital divide. While it is possible to enroll using
paper forms, the information is eventually input into a computer. Every state-run marketplace has a website, and Healthcare.gov is available for the other states. Users may expect information in print, but
there is very little available for consumers due to the newness of the

law, compared with the vast amounts of information available online. Librarians may have trouble locating or providing appropriate materials for low-level readers or those who have trouble using a computer.

6. **Provide the most complete information to answer the information request.** Health insurance questions can be complicated and time consuming. Consumers will have different options depending on their individual situation, and it will be the job of the librarian to gather all the necessary information from the patron during the reference interview and provide the most complete answer possible. Because of the complexity, it may be wise to break questions and answers into more manageable chunks. This allows the patron to absorb the information a step at a time, which reduces the possibility of being overwhelmed by too much information all at once. It also allows the librarian to determine the highest-priority aspects of the query, which can be answered first in the event the patron needs to return at a later time or wants to continue the search on his or her own. The goal should be to provide a complete answer to the question or provide appropriate resources that will help the consumer achieve his or her objective, such as going through the process of comparing options and enrolling in a plan.

7. **Do not provide advice or interpret health insurance information.** The role of the librarian should be understood by all staff. Librarians are trained information professionals, not health care providers or insurance experts. Health topics can be complex and difficult to understand, but it is vitally important not to interpret information for the consumer. By extension, the new health insurance law can create confusion and uncertainty for consumers. The library is a trusted place, and it is only natural that patrons may feel comfortable asking for advice, recommendations, or endorsements from library staff. Just as librarians are not able to provide legal or medical advice, it is never appropriate to provide health insurance advice. When confronted with this situation, librarians should inform the patron that they are able to facilitate access to resources, provide information, and make referrals; however, they are not able to provide interpretation or advice about health insurance matters. Libraries often use disclaimers when providing health information. The Consumer and Patient Health Information Section (CAPHIS) of MLA includes a statement about the purpose of disclaimers, which is to "inform patrons that libraries do not provide medical advice and do not interpret information for patrons." CAPHIS provides a discussion of this topic and sample disclaimer statements, which could be modified for health insurance information (available at http://caphis.mlanet.org/chis/disclaimers.html).

8. **Provide referrals when appropriate.** Many questions can be answered by information resources, glossaries, tax publications, or other

resources that are available at the library, but in some cases the appropriate response to certain health insurance questions will be a referral to outside agencies or professionals. For questions regarding advice or help choosing the best insurance plan, getting tax advice, or enrolling in a plan, connecting library users with community resources is the appropriate response. For help with choosing and enrolling in a plan, a directory of local navigator organizations can provide helpful contacts. In addition to providing referrals outside of the library, partnering with ACA experts, certified application counselors, and community organizations provides programming and service opportunities right at the library. Prior to and during enrollment periods, arrange for navigator organizations and certified application counselors to provide educational programs and enrollment assistance opportunities at the library. While librarians cannot make value judgments or recommendations of individual service providers or businesses, providing directories of local accountants, tax professionals, legal advisors, and other professionals may be useful to library patrons. When it is necessary to direct consumers to outside agencies or professionals, be clear that the referral is not a recommendation or endorsement of services. To aid patrons, point to guidelines and lists of questions to ask when choosing professional service providers; these resources are readily available online.

9. **Provide information in multiple formats, appropriate reading levels, and various languages (when available).** Gillaspy (2005) recommends providing health information in multiple formats for various learning styles, which can aid in understanding. For example, audio versions of health insurance information to supplement written information may be useful to library users. According to the ACA, insurance plans are also required to include plain language summaries and may provide additional easy-to-read health insurance materials. For example, the Kaiser Family Foundation provides an online video entitled "Health Insurance Explained" (http://kff.org/understanding-health-insurance).

10. **Maintain neutrality.** A final important consideration is to maintain neutrality when providing information. The topic of the Affordable Care Act, or Obamacare, can be politically charged, which underscores the imperative for library staff to provide nonbiased, authoritative information, regardless of personal opinions about the law. Depending on the sentiment of the community, the information about the legal requirements may be unpopular, and utilizing official sites will be the librarian's best approach.

HEALTH INSURANCE REFERENCE QUESTIONS

The ACA has brought attention to issues of health insurance coverage. For example, librarians may be assisting individuals that may currently lack health insurance (uninsured), have limited insurance (underinsured), or someone who is already covered by an employer (insured). The topic is multifaceted and complex; librarians will need to break down the reference questions into manageable parts to provide meaningful, understandable answers for users.

The Basics of Breaking Down a Health Insurance Question

The principles of health insurance reference closely mimic regular reference, with some key differences that will be explicated below. In the most basic terms, the first step is to inquire about who the information is for and how the information will be used. Then the topic areas are determined and the librarian finds appropriate resources and materials for the patron. The interaction concludes with a final check as to whether the question was answered satisfactorily.

Standard reference techniques apply. During the reference interaction, good listening skills and communicating for understanding are key to a successful outcome. Check back for understanding by restating not just what you heard but how you understand the question and what the patron hopes to receive in return. Watch for clues about literacy levels and other needs or preferences to determine appropriate resources. Locate and share resources, then check for validation; is it the right information? Does it answer the patron's question or solve the problem? Offer to provide additional help or services at a later time if more information is needed.

Step 1: Determine the Status of Requestor and How the Information Will Be Used

Who is the information for, and *how* will the information be used? (The patron or another person? An individual or a small business? A researcher or reporter? Do they have a special situation or belong to a special group or population?) For example, a person who needs assistance enrolling will be taken down a different path than a local news reporter who needs information about the enrollment process.

What information is needed? While it is impossible to imagine the totality of the questions that might be asked, some topics are predictable. For example, consumers will need to know definitions, important deadlines, and facts about the law. They may need help with finding plan information for comparison, costs, tax information, and even help with enrolling in a plan. Health insurance questions may also be complex, composed of several components making up the full inquiry.

Where does the person reside? This is important when the question is about enrollment or choosing a plan since these differ from state to state. The patron may be asking for information on behalf of someone else, so this is a necessary piece of information.

How does the person prefer to receive the information? Inquire about the desired source and output format: print or online? Are they comfortable using the computer?

As you gather information, listen carefully and verify with the patron your understanding of the question.

Step 2: Determine the Broad Topic Area(s)

The Affordable Care Act is a multifaceted and complex law. Understanding some of the broad topic areas below will help librarians break health insurance questions into manageable chunks. The following is a sampling of the many topics and subtopics that might generate questions about the ACA.

Basic information:

- Benefits and coverage
- Preventive services
- Terminology
- Metal tiered system (bronze, silver, gold, platinum)

Individual mandate:

- Deadlines
- Tax information
- Requirements, penalties, subsidies
- Triggers for special enrollment period
- Changes in coming years

Exchange and marketplace information:

- Federally facilitated exchange (Healthcare.gov)
- Exchanges, marketplaces by state, state-specific info

Insurance plans through the ACA:

- Available insurance plans (state specific)
- Dental insurance

- Shopping, comparing

Enrollment help:

- Enrollment options (computer, phone, paper form)
- Help with enrollment
- Navigator and enrollment counselor organizations
- Directories of community organizations

About the ACA:

- Statistics, news
- Reports in the media
- Verification or evaluation of information in the media
- Politics of the ACA
- Other aspects of the ACA (such as requirements for nonprofit entities)

Legislation:

- About the Patient Protection and Affordable Care Act
- Health care reform in general

Other insurance programs:

- Small Business Health Options Program (SHOP)
- Medicaid state expansion
- Medicaid and CHIP
- Medicare
- Veterans Administration Tricare
- Managed care plans (e.g., HMO or PPO)
- Other (long-term care insurance, flexible spending accounts (FSAs), managed care plans)

Step 3: Determine Resources for Topic Area and Specific Situation

The majority of resources will be online, and library staff should always choose authoritative sites. It is worth noting that in most if not all states, there will be two health insurance exchange sites; one site will be the consumer site for enrolling in a plan, and the other will be the official state government site for insurance matters. Typically, resources about insurance regulations, navigator organizations, partner resources, and other nonconsumer information will be on the state government sites. The corresponding federal example is the consumer-oriented Healthcare.gov site and the health insurance marketplace site from the Centers for Medicare and Medicaid Services, https://marketplace.cms.gov/. Familiarity with the relevant sites in a particular state will prepare library staff with the resources for many ACA questions. Unfortunately, copycat sites have popped up in many states that have similar names and website addresses; typically these sites contain biased or politically motivated information. The sites are cleverly designed to look like the state marketplace site, but digging deep uncovers verbiage that is clearly biased. Also, the ACA triggered opportunities for marketplace fraud. Librarians can help patrons evaluate sites and watch for red flags that might indicate fraudulent information or activities. As a solid starting point, the MedlinePlus "Health Insurance" page is a current compilation of authoritative health insurance resources (http://medlineplus.gov/healthinsurance/).

Based on patron preferences and needs, the librarian may need to provide materials in an easy-to-understand format, which can include plain language materials or multimedia resources. Fortunately, the ACA includes a provision that insurance plans must provide an easy-to-understand summary about the plan's benefits and coverage (http://www.hhs.gov/healthcare/rights/sbc/index.html).

In library communities where other languages are spoken, patrons will benefit from multilingual materials. Healthcare.gov provides a separate site in Spanish (https://cuidadodesalud.gov) in addition to information in languages other than English. For states that have their own exchanges, information is available online and by telephone to reflect the languages spoken by the major ethnic groups within the state. For example, the health insurance exchange in Hawaii provides customer support in several Asian and Pacific Islander languages in addition to native Hawaiian, whereas the New York exchange provides materials in seventeen languages, including Yiddish and Haitian Creole.

As mentioned previously, a referral can be the appropriate resource or answer. When a patron needs enrollment advice or professional services related to insurance, knowing the appropriate type of service or organization will be required, such as accountants or tax preparers, enrollment counselors, and community organizations. The skilled librarian will be able to sort out which questions are answerable and when it is appropriate to direct a patron to services and resources from other organizations or professionals.

Step 4: Verify Results with Consumer

The final step of the insurance reference transaction is the verification stage and the conclusion of the transaction. Due to the nature of health insurance questions, the librarian may not know if the furnished information answered the patron's question adequately. Many insurance questions will be broken into subqueries, and it is possible that more than one staff member will interact with a particular patron. Whenever possible, verify with the patron that the information provided was appropriate, understandable, and useful. Asking open-ended questions such as "How helpful was this information in addressing your question?" will identify any remaining questions or additional needs, thus providing an opportunity to serve the patron fully.

TRAINING FOR LIBRARY STAFF

The ACA is shining a spotlight on libraries as a place to get help with enrolling in health insurance. By extension, libraries may start to see an increase in public awareness of services in general and, in particular, about reference services related to health information and insurance questions. Given the constant changes in the health and medical field, library staff will benefit from ongoing training about health literacy and consumer health information services in general, including health insurance and the ACA. Training is essential to keep up to date with resources, to replace lost knowledge due to staff turnover, and to learn about how consumers use new technologies to access information and improve their own health.

With regard to the ACA, all staff who interact with library patrons should be informed about relevant resources and best practices for responding to health insurance inquiries. While emphasis is put on health insurance leading up to and during the annual enrollment period, library staff should be prepared for questions at any time of the year. For instance, knowing in advance about special circumstances and life events that trigger eligibility for special enrollment will keep staff ready and able to help. At the very least, staff must know about the marketplace in their own state, be knowledgeable about important deadlines, and know where to find information to answer a range of questions. Maintaining a current directory of local navigator organizations and certified application counselors is highly recommended for all libraries.

The complexity of health insurance issues draws attention to literacy levels and the need for easy-to-understand materials. Training about issues of health literacy and health insurance literacy will provide library staff essential tools for working with all patrons, not just those with lower literacy levels. Training and resources are available through state libraries, the regional NN/LM offices, and other library training organizations. A few notable resources include WebJunction's "Health Happens in Libraries" initiative, which offers a blog, ongoing webinars, and resources about health and health insurance topics for libraries (http://www.webjunction.org/explore-topics/ehealth.html).

There may be training or resources for libraries at the state level as well. For instance, the Covered California Library Toolkit is an exceptional resource for training, public outreach, and programming that could be used as a model in other states (http://hbex.coveredca.com/PDFs/style-guides/Library%20Toolkit-FINAL%2011-14.pdf). Check with the state library and the health insurance exchange (if one exists) to discover training resources specific to your state.

Reasons to keep current:

- The law will phase in new requirements, benefits, and other conditions that will impact users each subsequent year through 2020.
- The current law may change, depending on changes in political parties and governmental actions.
- The field of medicine is constantly changing with new discoveries and research results.
- Users are accessing health information through new technologies and social media; librarians can help users understand the issues and make good decisions.

EMOTIONAL LABOR AND REFERENCE WORK

Emotional labor is "present in all types of library work and often places an invisible, but demanding, burden on library workers" (Matteson and Miller 2014, 106). In particular, library users may seek information for health issues that are sensitive, personal, and emotional. For example, health concerns may be serious or life altering, such as receiving a new diagnosis (NN/LM 2015). As such, we must acknowledge the aspects of emotional labor involved in health reference work.

The emotional and personal nature of health information requests can especially place emotional demands on library staff. Emotional labor deals with "the challenges associated with expressing the appropriate emotions as required by workplace or supervisor expectations" (Matteson and Miller 2014, 96). An example of emotional labor in health insurance reference work might be when a librarian is assisting someone and the individual determines that they fall in the "coverage gap," meaning the individual makes too much money to qualify for Medicaid but not enough to qualify for the marketplace. Therefore, training, resources, and organizational support are critical for library positions "inherently prone to emotional labor situations" (Matteson and Miller 2014, 103). In light of the ACA, health care reform in general and making important decisions about health insurance plans and benefits can elicit strong emotions. Hence, we must also recognize "emotional labor" aspects of reference work in the provision of health insurance information.

To help prepare library staff with coping strategies for the emotional demands of reference work, libraries can implement training for staff about appropriate responses to health references questions. In addition, managers can balance reference work schedules "to give employees the chance to replenish their emotional resources" (Matteson and Miller 2014, 103). Given the emotional situations involved in reference work, a number of strategies can help library staff effectively cope with the personal and emotional nature of health reference transactions.

SUMMARY

The Affordable Care Act presents exciting opportunities for librarians, including public librarians, hospital librarians, and academic health sciences librarians, to connect communities with information about health, health insurance plans, and policies affecting public health. This chapter addresses a number of areas relevant to providing health insurance information. In light of recent health care reforms, guidelines for consumer health reference services have been expanded to reflect the emerging role of librarians in supporting health insurance inquiries. A step-by-step approach to working with health insurance questions is also discussed. As the number of people enrolling in health plans continues to grow, this chapter provides advice for librarians in helping patrons navigate the evolving health care landscape.

REFERENCES

American Library Association. 2013. "ALA President Releases Statement on Libraries and the Affordable Care Act." http://www.ala.org/news/press-releases/2013/07/ala-president-releases-statement-libraries-and-affordable-care-act.

CAPHIS. 1996. "The Librarian's Role in the Provision of Consumer Health Information and Patient Education." http://caphis.mlanet.org/chis/librarian.html.

Gillaspy, Mary. 2005. "Factors Affecting the Provision of Consumer Health Information in Public Libraries: The Last Five Years." *Library Trends* 53(3):480–95.

Goldsmith, Francisca . 2015. *Libraries and the Affordable Care Act: Helping the Community Understand Health-Care Options.* Chicago: American Library Association.

Harris, Roma, et al. 2010. "I'm Not Sure If That's What Their Job Is: Consumer Health Information and Emerging 'Healthwork' Roles in the Public Library." *Reference & User Services Quarterly* 49(3):239–52.

Linnan, Laura, et al. 2004. "Public Libraries as a Resource for Promoting Health: Results from the Health for Everyone in Libraries Project (HELP) Librarian Survey." *Health Promotion Practice* 5(2):182–90.

Matteson, Miriam. and Shelly Miller. 2014. "What Library Managers Should Know about Emotional Labor." *Public Library Quarterly* 33(2):95–107.

Murray, Susan. 2008. "Consumer Health Information Services in Public Libraries in Canada and the US." *Journal of the Canadian Health Libraries Association* 29(4):141–43.

NN/LM. 2015. "Consumer Health Reference Interview and Ethical Issues." http://nnlm.gov/outreach/consumer/ethics.html.

RESOURCES HIGHLIGHTED IN CHAPTER

"Covered California Library Toolkit" from Covered California. Helpful guidelines for library outreach; part of the Partner Toolkit page. Online at http://hbex.coveredca.com/toolkit/.

"Glossary" from Healthcare.gov. An essential resource with definitions of insurance-related words and phrases to help users understand the terminology. Online at https://www.healthcare.gov/glossary.

Healthinsurance.org. Provides consumer information about affordable health and medical coverage for all states. Online at http://www.healthinsurance.org/.

"Health Insurance Marketplace" from the Centers for Medicare and Medicaid Services. Online at https://marketplace.cms.gov.

"Health Insurance Marketplace Calculator" from the Kaiser Family Foundation. Online at http://kff.org/interactive/subsidy-calculator/.

MedlinePlus "Health Insurance" page. Current compilation of authoritative health insurance resources. Online at http://medlineplus.gov/healthinsurance/.

"State by State" from the U.S. Department of Health and Human Services. Online at http://www.hhs.gov/healthcare/facts/bystate/statebystate.html.

"Understanding Health Insurance" from the Kaiser Family Foundation. Includes videos, quiz, zip-code-specific data, information in Spanish, and more. Online at http://kff.org/understanding-health-insurance/?utm_source=kff&utm_medium=tile&utm_content=home&utm_campaign=consumer.

WebJunction Health Happens in Libraries. Provides a range of resources for public libraries supporting community health and wellness. Online at http://www.webjunction.org/explore-topics/ehealth.html.

Chapter Five

Current Practices in Health Insurance Information Provision

Emily Vardell

This chapter presents original research conducted to explore the services librarians are providing to support Affordable Care Act (ACA) information needs. These large-scale trends paint a picture of current practices, provide evidence that librarians are involved in this arena, and indicate gaps that may be opportunities for new, in-depth initiatives. These results include a discussion of the types of questions asked as well as proactive services librarians are providing. These larger trends are then explored in greater depth in the following chapter, which focuses on individual case studies to provide further elaboration.

HEALTH INSURANCE INFORMATION SEEKING IN CONTEXT

Health insurance information seeking and use occurs in a variety of contexts, including human resources departments, health care providers' offices, social services departments, insurance broker firms, and libraries. While previous studies have evaluated aspects of health insurance literacy (as outlined in chapter 3 of this book), there have been no studies to date of the provision and use of health insurance information in a library setting.

Clearly, there is a need for assistance when evaluating health insurance information and making related decisions regarding health insurance coverage options. Yin et al. (2009) demonstrated low levels of ability to complete health insurance forms and calculate the annual cost of a health insurance policy. Evaluations of both public assistance informational materials (Pati et al. 2012; Wallace, DeVoe, and Hansen 2011) as well as health insurance companies' promotional and informational materials (Vardell 2013; McCormack et al. 2009) have demonstrated that these summary of benefits and coverage forms are not written with low-literacy users in mind. If insurance materials continue to be written at higher-grade reading levels, there will be a need for information professionals to point to supplementary resources and advocate for new standards in health insurance materials.

Access to health insurance and health care coverage are key in addressing health status disparities. A recent study of citizens in Massachusetts demonstrated overall improvements in individuals' self-assessed health following Massachusetts health care reform, which required universal coverage of all citizens (Courtemanche and Zapata 2014). Physical health, mental health, joint disorders, and body mass index were all demonstrated to improve following health care reform. In addition, the improvements were strongest for people with lower incomes, nonwhites, and near-elderly adults, many of whom have been more greatly affected by health disparities.

This initial study by Courtemache and Zapata demonstrates promise for health care reform as a method for reducing health care disparities. Health insurance information seeking is an important precursor to effective health care reform. As summarized by the U.S. Department of Health and Human Services (2008), "the success of health system reform will depend in large part on the capacity of individuals, families, and communities to make informed decisions about their health."

HEALTH INSURANCE INFORMATION SEEKING IN LIBRARIES: THE CALL TO ACTION

Following the passage and implementation of the Affordable Care Act, librarians are more frequently called upon to provide assistance with navigating the health insurance marketplace and understanding health insurance terminology and forms. In a call to action at the 2013 American Library Association Conference, President Barack Obama requested help from librarians in assisting the public with this new phase of health insurance in the United States (Wright 2013). Libraries offer an ideal context for health insurance information seeking, as librarians have traditionally assisted with completing public assistance forms and are well trained in ascertaining and meeting information needs. While offering assistance with navigating the insurance process is an emerging and important service, there have been no published studies on librarians assisting with health insurance information seeking. This lack of published evidence suggests further research is necessary to explore trends and best practices in this area.

CURRENT PRACTICES RESEARCH STUDY DESIGN

To explore how librarians—in particular, health sciences librarians—are meeting the needs of those seeking information about the Affordable Care Act or health insurance, a two-phase study was conducted. The study began with a large-scale qualitative and quantitative survey and continued with a smaller-scale semistructured interview study.

In order to capture the communication between librarians and individuals interested in health insurance information, a survey was administered to health sciences librarians (see table 5.1 for survey questions). The survey was designed to capture the variety of ways librarians have addressed this information need with a focus on information exchanges following the implementation of the Affordable Care Act. The survey included questions regarding the type of library in which the respondent worked (e.g., health sciences library, public library, hospital library); whether the librarian had created information portals on health insurance information (e.g., LibGuide); and the number of patron queries the librarian had answered, with which kind of patron (e.g., health care provider, student, general public), using which resources to answer these questions. The analysis of survey responses includes differences in types of libraries (e.g., academic, hospital, public), as well as an exploration of the interpersonal communication between librarian and patron.

SETTING THE STAGE

This study focused specifically on the services provided by health sciences librarians. Health sciences librarians are well poised to fill a multitude of roles in the provision of Affordable Care Act information (as outlined by Malachowski in chapter 2 of this book), and the survey was developed and administered specifically to study this population. The survey was administered to health sciences librarians through distribution to popular medical library listservs (e.g., MEDLIB-L and regional Medical Library Association listservs such as MACMLA-L), Twitter (#medlibs), and Facebook. A total of 222 respondents began the survey, with 191 complete responses. The majority of the 222 respondents worked at academic health sciences libraries (45 percent) or hospital libraries (36 percent), with fewer respondents from other types of academic libraries (9 percent), special/corporate libraries (2 percent), public libraries (2 percent), and other (6 percent). Figure 5.1 demonstrates that while more responses were collected from academic health science librarians, more hospital librarians actually reported answering an ACA-related question.

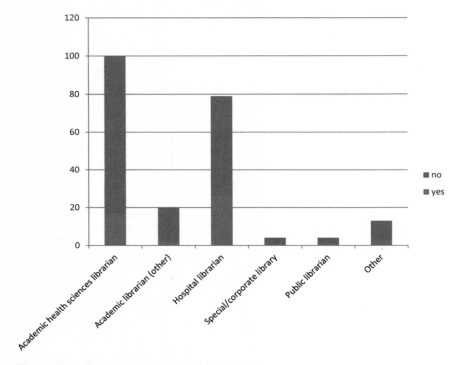

Figure 5.1.   Question Demand by Library Type (n = 222).

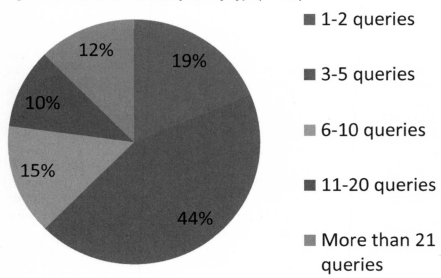

Figure 5.2.   Number of Reference Queries (n = 48).

Overall, fifty respondents (23 percent) stated they had provided individual assistance to patron(s) interested in health insurance information, and many reported multiple reference queries (see figure 5.2). These results clearly suggest that there are some librarians who are frequent providers of health insurance information assistance.

Those librarians who had provided health insurance information (n = 48) also reported working with a wide variety of patron types, the most common being the general public (n = 35, see figure 5.3). Other frequently reported categories included staff/employees (n = 21), patients (n = 12), and students (n = 11). Figure 5.3 also demonstrates which patron types were most common for each of the library types. For example, patients and hospital administrators were a more common type of patron asking an ACA-related question in hospital libraries. Academic health science librarians indicated that the general public, staff/employees, students, and faculty were more commonly the patrons asking questions.

Survey respondents were invited to list the proactive ACA information services they had provided. Thirty-eight respondents (17 percent) reported creating an ACA information portal (e.g., LibGuide). Other respondents reported writing newsletter content for affiliates, sending emails with helpful links, and providing training for other librarians (these strategies are further explored in chapter 2, focused on the roles librarians can play, and chapter 6, which highlights best practices in the field). Respondents expressed concern in regarding bias in available ACA information, as well as pressure from city

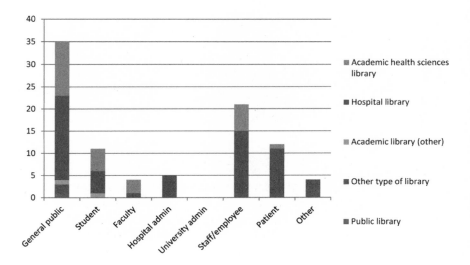

Figure 5.3.   Type of Patron by Library Type (n = 49).

government, hospital administration, and other overseeing bodies to limit the amount of help provided.

When prompted to name their favorite resource on health insurance information, 36 percent listed Healthcare.gov as their favorite. Other favorites included state-specific health insurance exchange sites (11 percent), librarian-created information portals (7 percent), Department of Health and Human Services sites (7 percent), MedlinePlus (5.5 percent), the Kaiser Family Foundation (5.5 percent), and a variety of other resources (27 percent).

The qualitative section of the survey also invited participants to outline the most frequent reference interview exchanges (as modeled in figure 5.4). The survey offered short answer boxes for respondents to list the patron type, medium, question, recommended resources, and any other notes. The responses can be modeled as falling into two categories: the questions asked by the general public/patient and questions asked by an institutional affiliate. Questions presented by the general public or patients were about the Affordable Care Act in general or specifically enrollment in health insurance. Librarians shared their recommendations for these questions, which included a variety of information sources as well as referrals to other individuals who might offer alternative sources of information.

The second most frequently reported type of reference question fell under the category of institutional affiliate. In this case, a student, researcher, physician, administrator, or quality improvement consultant approached the librarian requesting resources/data for an ACA-related publication or professional

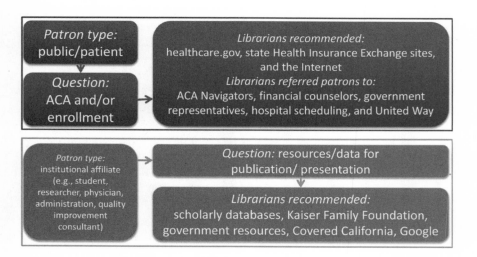

Figure 5.4. The Two Types of Most Frequently Reported Reference Interview Exchanges.

presentation. The recommendations presented by librarians answering this type of question were a little more homogenous, often peer-reviewed or government-funded resources on the topic.

The variety of recommended approaches outlined by the librarians may be reflective of the diversity of patron questions posed at the desk. The differences may also suggest that additional training could be offered to provide guidance on concrete approaches librarians could take in responding to these types of questions. In addition to step-by-step guides (such as the recommended steps posed by Charbonneau and Ham in chapter 4 of this text), librarians may be interested in additional training opportunities. This conclusion was supported by the survey responses collected (see figure 5.5). While "none" was not one of the available options to the question "Did you participate in any training on this topic?," many participants wrote in "none" under "other," with one participant writing, "No, but would have liked to have had some training."

In summary, although only 23 percent of participants stated they had answered an insurance-related question, of those fifty respondents, over 80 percent reported answering three questions or more. The most commonly reported reference queries demonstrate two types of information needs— those of the general public and those of researchers/health care providers. Based on the survey responses, ten librarians were selected for follow-up interviews to collect additional information on the interpersonal communica-

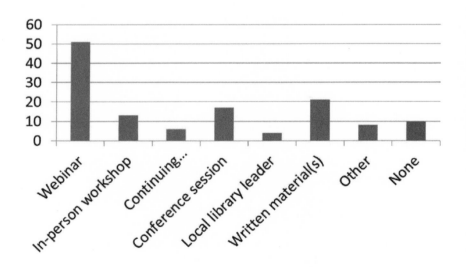

Figure 5.5. Participation in Training on ACA/Health Insurance Information (n = 92).

tion between librarian and patron. Highlights from findings from these interviews are presented as profiles in best practices in the next chapter.

Survey Questions

In what kind of library do you work?

- Academic health sciences library
- Academic library (other)
- Hospital library
- Special/corporate library
- Public library
- Other: _____

Did your library create an information portal (e.g., LibGuide) with resources designed to provide assistance understanding/navigating the Affordable Care Act?

- Yes. If so, please paste link here: _____
- No
- I'm not sure.

Have you provided individual assistance to a patron/patrons interested in health insurance information (including, but not limited to, understanding the Affordable Care Act, finding insurance in the healthcare marketplace, understanding health insurance terminology, etc.)?

- Yes
- No

If yes, how many reference queries related to health insurance have you responded to?

- 1–2 queries
- 3–5 queries
- 6–10 queries
- 11–20 queries
- More than 21 queries

What were the types of patrons asking for assistance with health insurance information? (Please check all that apply.)

- General public

- Student
- Faculty
- Hospital administration
- Staff/employee
- Patient
- Other: _____

If no, are you aware of colleagues at your library who have assisted with this kind of question?

- Yes. If so, you are invited to list the email(s) of librarians who have responded to health insurance queries, as appropriate: _____
- No

What is your favorite resource on health insurance information and/or the Affordable Care Act? (not a required question)

- Paste link or title here: _____

Did you participate in any training on this topic? (Please check all that apply.)

- Webinar
- In-person workshop
- Continuing education (CE) course
- Conference session
- Local library leader
- Written material(s)
- Other: _____

Optional: please describe one of the health insurance reference questions/interviews you responded to. Please include information about the patron, the medium in which it was conducted (e.g., face-to-face, email, phone), the question, and the resources you recommended.

I will be conducting follow-up interviews with librarians to obtain additional information about this topic. If you are available and interested in being interviewed about health insurance information, please leave your email here:

_____

Additional comments/questions:

REFERENCES

Courtemanche, C. J., and D. Zapata. 2014. "Does Universal Coverage Improve Health? The Massachusetts Experience." *Journal of Policy Analysis and Management* 33(1):36–69.

McCormack, L., C. Bann, J. Uhrig, N. Berkman, and R. Rudd. 2009. "Health Insurance Literacy of Older Adults." *Journal of Consumer Affairs* 43(2):223–48.

Pati, S., J. E. Kavanagh, S. K. Bhatt, A. T. Wong, K. Noonan, and A. Cnaan. 2012. "Reading Level of Medicaid Renewal Applications." *Academic Pediatrics* 12(4):297–301.

U.S. Department of Health and Human Services. 2008. "America's Health Literacy: Why We Need Accessible Health Information." Issue Brief.

Vardell, E. 2013. "Readability Levels of Health Insurance Summary of Benefits and Coverage Forms." Paper presented at the annual conference of the Medical Library Association, Boston, May.

Wallace, L. S., J. E. DeVoe, and J. S. Hansen. 2011. "Assessment of Children's Public Health Insurance Program Enrollment Applications: A Health Literacy Perspective." *Journal of Pediatric Health Care* 25(2):133–37.

Wright, J. 2013. "Breaking News: President Obama to Reveal Message to ALA Conference." *District Dispatch*, June 27. http://www.districtdispatch.org/2013/06/breaking-news-president-obama-to-reveal-message-to-ala-conference/.

Yin, H. S., M. Johnson, A. L. Mendelsohn, M. A. Abrams, L. M. Sanders, and B. P. Dreyer. 2009. "The Health Literacy of Parents in the United States: A Nationally Representative Study." *Pediatrics* 124 (Suppl. 3): S289–98.

Chapter Six

Profiles in Health Insurance Information Provision Best Practices

Emily Vardell

This chapter presents the results of semistructured interviews conducted with librarians who provide Affordable Care Act (ACA) or health insurance information services (see the appendix at the end of this chapter for the interview guide). These profiles offer examples of the kinds of services librarians are providing in this arena and are presented as potential springboards for librarians seeking to enrich their information resources and services regarding the Affordable Care Act. Many of these ideas can be implemented in a wide variety of settings building on the kinds of work already being done in the library.

While all of these profiles focus specifically on the innovative projects librarians have undertaken regarding the Affordable Care Act, these strategies can be applied to a variety of special topics pertinent to health sciences librarianship. For example, Kay Hogan Smith and Mary Ellen Nolan, as information mediator and programming host, respectively, provide excellent examples of how preestablished partnerships can be enriched through focused projects, in this case regarding the Affordable Care Act. The profiles for Michele Malloy, Lisa Kilburn, and Paul Levett provide concrete examples of the unique aspects of research, presentation, and embedded clinical support for Affordable Care Act information needs. Finally, as a librarian advocate, Michelle Kraft presents a compelling argument for the importance of highlighting the value of the library in supporting Affordable Care Act implementation locally at your institution.

KAY HOGAN SMITH, MLS, MPH, AHIP

Community services librarian and director of Health InfoNet of Alabama
Lister Hill Library, University of Alabama at Birmingham (UAB)
Website: https://www.uab.edu/lister/staff-directory?userID=12&cat-
  id=0&id=24

Information Mediator at a Glance

- Builds partnerships with public librarians and community organizations to support dissemination and use of quality health information
- Assists public librarians seeking authoritative resources to address ACA information needs
- Emails notices to public librarians about training opportunities
- Locates information on coverage tiers for patients and refers to community clinics that provide free care
- Assists faith-based organizations with setting up enrollment events with trained navigators

Kay Hogan Smith, Information Mediator Profile. Photo courtesy of Kay Hogan Smith.

Information Mediator Profile

Kay Hogan Smith works at an academic health sciences library as both the liaison to the public health school and the community outreach librarian. In her outreach efforts, she partners with public librarians, faith-based organizations, and community organizations to distribute and encourage the use of reliable health information. She also helps support an adjunct library strictly for patients at the UAB ambulatory care center by providing health information directly to consumers.

As an information mediator, Kay has received many questions from public librarians getting asked by patrons about health insurance enrollment. When a public librarian is confronted with a difficult ACA question, they often turn to Kay for support and recommendations. The public librarians are pleased to receive recommended resources from Kay, who also passes along training opportunities to the librarians (specifically the Health Happens in Libraries program, available at http://www.webjunction.org/explore-topics/ehealth.html). Kay also attends enrollment events sponsored by a local non-profit navigator group, where she supplements the support being offered by telling people about sources for general health information.

Kay also works with community organizations with which she already has well-established partnerships. For example, she has worked with health ministers at community churches to hold enrollment events with one-on-one navigator assistance. In addition, she proactively passes pertinent information along to her contacts at these organizations and uses them as an information source when she has questions.

In her role as a consumer health librarian at the UAB ambulatory care center patient library, she has received referrals from other hospital departments to help individuals obtain information about their insurance options. Most of the individuals that she interacts with there have minimal computer skills and require a lot of assistance. To answer these questions, Kay refers individuals to the navigators at Enroll Alabama, or she calls on the patron's behalf with specific questions. Some individual navigators have developed charts that lay out how much you need to make to qualify for different types of coverages/subsidies. Unfortunately, Kay reports that these questions can be quite difficult to manage, as many of the patrons fall in the coverage gap where they make too much to qualify for Medicaid and too little to qualify for subsidies. To offer some alternative options, Kay refers people to community clinics that provide free care. This information is available through Health InfoNet of Alabama, where Kay has a database of free clinics (http://www.healthinfonet.org/).

As an information mediator, Kay has the connections in place to facilitate two-way information exchanges between the general public and those who can provide targeted, one-on-one assistance. As Kay underscores, "it's important for librarians to be involved in this. There are people out there that have a need. It is a good place for us to be useful."

MARY ELLEN NOLAN, MLS, AHIP

Consumer health librarian
New Hanover County Public Library, Wilmington, North Carolina
Website: http://nhcpl.libguides.com/prf.php?account_id=6433

Programming Host at a Glance

• Proactively builds connections with relevant organizations
• Collects relevant literature from these organizations and trusted websites
• Provides a space for both individual help and group programming
• Invites authoritative speakers to present on a range of topics, from individual enrollment to the employer mandate

Programming Host Profile

Mary Ellen works at the only dedicated consumer health library in a public library in North Carolina. In her role, Mary Ellen manages the consumer health department of her public library, including collection development, reference services, and health-related programming. When she came into this role three years ago, she took the time to reach out to relevant health organizations in the area. Having these connections in place helped her hit the ground running once the Affordable Care Act was in place and programming was essential.

   To provide Affordable Care Act information services, Mary Ellen partners with two agencies with trained navigators: one is MedNorth, a Medicare/Medicaid clinic, and the other is Legal Aid of North Carolina. New Hanover County's consumer health library department provides a quiet, private space for individuals from these organizations to meet one-on-one with people requiring assistance with Affordable Care Act insurance enrollment. Representatives from MedNorth met with people in this space and also circulated around the library, approaching individuals and asking if they needed assistance with enrollment. Representatives from Legal Aid met with individuals on an appointment-only basis at the library. ACA-related sessions took place in multiple branches within the New Hanover County public library system. Mary Ellen reports that the sessions held in the library branch that serves a population with a lower socioeconomic status, as well as sessions held on weekends, were the most well attended, underscoring the importance of knowing your audience and distributing resources accordingly.

In addition to one-on-one assistance, these organizations provided specific resources that Mary Ellen printed out and displayed on a table within the consumer health library, along with information from Healthcare.gov. Having the printed information available within this space was a popular way for people to obtain information without necessarily having to ask directly for it. Mary Ellen reports printing out information on a regular basis as the piles of paper depleted.

When people request one-on-one reference assistance from Mary Ellen (outside of these programming events), she shares the collected, printed literature with the patrons; points them to Healthcare.gov; and then refers them to MedNorth and Legal Aid, as needed. She stresses that as she is not a trained navigator, she does not assist them with enrolling in health insurance.

Mary Ellen's active recruiting of individuals and organizations that could provide one-on-one and group assistance with the Affordable Care Act is an excellent example of how a librarian can serve as a programming host. In addition, her proactive measures in locating the movers and shakers in the area prior to the information need underscores the importance of laying groundwork in advance.

MICHELE MALLOY, MALS

Research services coordinator
Dahlgren Memorial Library at Georgetown University Medical Center, Washington, DC
Website: http://dml.georgetown.edu/

Research Support at a Glance

- Provides one-on-one assistance to patrons creating presentations or seeking answers to health care administration questions
- Encourages the use of a multitude of resources, including gray literature, to research insurance-related topics
- Uses clinician contacts for help with terminology and clarifying questions when needed

Research Support Profile

When Michele Malloy was interviewed for this project, she was the research services coordinator at the Dahlgren Memorial Library at Georgetown University Medical Center. This library primarily serves the medical school, but they also serve undergraduate and graduate students at the School of Nursing and Health Studies and an affiliated hospital.

Michele Malloy, Research Support Profile. Photo courtesy of Michele Malloy.

While Michele shares that Affordable Care Act concerns are "not our biggest question," the questions they do receive are more geared toward the provider, particularly those who wish to be better informed when talking with their patients. This includes questions from medical and nursing students who wish to be better informed or perhaps are in charge of creating an ACA-related presentation. Michele notes that questions from practicing clinicians are often posed directly following a webinar or conference, where the clinician returns with follow-up research questions.

Michelle offers two examples to illustrate the different types of ACA-related questions that she has answered. The first was from students in a postbaccalaureate, premedical program for underrepresented populations. For this program, students are required to complete an exploration project, where they are given a topic, do extensive research, and give a two-hour presentation to their colleagues. For the last three years, students have had questions regarding the Affordable Care Act from a variety of perspectives, including administrative and clinical. As this project's liaison, Michele worked closely with these students to address these rather topics. She helped them collect information broadly about the project and then select specific aspects to present as examples.

The second reference example that Michele shares is from a patron re-questing research help about how individuals with dual eligibility for both Medicaid and Medicare might be impacted by the ACA. Michele highlights an important aspect of researching this topic in that most of the information was from the gray literature, whereas "the published literature is really just highlighting the problem instead of offering any guidelines that are helpful." While Michele's research uncovered gray literature for patient resources, the lack of clinical, published resources answering the dual-eligibility question led to the creation of an institutional task force to develop guidelines for this. Because of positive word-of-mouth, Michelle continued to receive more questions about the ramifications of the ACA, and through this experience and working with patrons, her expertise in this area has grown.

While she mostly uses online content, including gray literature, to respond to ACA reference requests, she has also relied on her preestablished clinician contacts as information resources. These individuals can provide direction on what terminology is being used and what questions are being asked. This information can be used to refine the help that is provided by reference librarians.

Underscoring the key role that librarians can play in this area, Michele concludes "providers don't know what to ask" and may not know where to search for information. As a research support librarian, "this is a great opportunity for us to become knowledgeable and share that knowledge."

LISA KILBURN, MLS

Information resource specialist
Southern Regional Area Health Education Center (SR-AHEC), Fayette-
    ville, North Carolina
Website: http://www.southernregionalahec.org/

Presentation Support at a Glance

- Locates authoritative ACA information in a systematic manner
- Stays current on health care policy through email alerts and reviewing top-quality literature (i.e., the "Health Policy and Reform" and "Medicine and Society" sections of the *New England Journal of Medicine*)

Presentation Support Profile

Lisa Kilburn serves as the information resource specialist at the Southern Regional AHEC of North Carolina, which serves as the main medical library for a nine-county region. While the AHEC is open to the public, the medical library staff most heavily serves the family medicine residency program based at the AHEC.

In the collected survey responses (see chapter 5 of this book) and interviews conducted for this chapter, several librarians reported assisting patrons seeking to create presentations on the Affordable Care Act for different constituencies. Lisa provides an excellent example of how this type of research support looks in practice.

She describes how one of the AHEC quality improvement (QI) consultants came to the library and shared that he was tasked with creating a

Lisa Kilburn, Presentation Support Profile. Photo courtesy of Lisa Kilburn.

presentation for a group of physicians on the Affordable Care Act. While the QI consultant was familiar with the Act, he sought out Lisa's assistance with compiling high-quality information in a more systematic way. He was interested in locating examples of PowerPoint presentations others had created on the ACA on which to base his presentation. Most of the existing material focused on employers' duties under the ACA, but Lisa was able to locate some examples that focused specifically on the QI's needs, which centered on the physician's perspective and how it was likely to impact this population.

In addition, Lisa directed the patron to the extensive articles on health care policy available from the *New England Journal of Medicine*, particularly the "Health Policy and Reform" and "Medicine and Society" sections. Lisa also reports signing up for regular email updates from these and similar sources to stay up to date on health care policy. Her background knowledge in this area was helpful when she was tasked with supporting a patron seeking assistance in developing a high-quality, authoritative presentation on the ACA.

PAUL LEVETT, MSC, MA ED.

Reference and instruction librarian
Himmelfarb Health Sciences Library, George Washington University (GWU), Washington, DC
Website: http://himmelfarb.gwu.edu

Embedded Clinical Support at a Glance

- Attends case-study tutorials with first-year medical students
- Encourages students to consider medication pricing concerns faced by patients with different types of insurance coverage
- Promotes the institutional repository as a method of hosting Affordable Care Act research taking place at his institution

Embedded Clinical Support Profile

Paul serves as a reference and instruction librarian at the Himmelfarb Health Sciences Library, an academic medical library. Librarians are embedded in the first year of the medical school curriculum and also teach students in the public health and nursing programs.

Paul has the opportunity to sit in on small-group, case-study tutorials with first-year medical students. When the discussion turns toward drug therapies that may be prescribed, Paul encourages the students to consider whether a

Paul Levett, Embedded Clinical Support Profile. Photo courtesy of Paul Levett.

patient can afford the prescribed medication. He asks students to keep the patient's age, income level, and health insurance status in mind when determining whether the medication will be affordable. Paul points students to the relevant websites with state and federal income guidelines for public assistance (i.e., Medicare, Medicaid, and CHIP, the Children's Health Insurance Program) and discusses the coverage gap for those who do not qualify. When considering some of the differences between insurers and what they cover, drugs can be looked up by brand name in Fingertip Formulary (http://www.fingertipformulary.com) to identify what tier a drug occupies for a particular insurance plan in a particular state. A patient could be asked to contact their health insurer to find out what co-pay or percent co-insurance is required to be paid by the patient for each tier of the insurer's prescription formulary. For the cost of drugs, Paul recommends consulting the *Medical Letter on Drugs and Therapeutics*, which provides the retail cost of a thirty-day supply. It is then possible to work out roughly what the cost to the patient of a course of drug therapy may be. As an example offered by Paul, if the insurer reimburses 25 percent of the cost of tier 7 on-patent drugs and the co-insurance is 75 percent, and the cost of an eight-week course of the drug Humira (used to treat Crohn's disease) is $4,682, this would cost the patient approximately $1,755 each month until they reached their annual out-of-pocket limit.

While he also encourages students to consider the coverage an insurer provides, he admits that individual policy-level information is often not published by insurers nor readily available, but this type of classroom exercise can be used to illustrate the wider point that clinicians may go beyond thinking about whether a drug is therapeutically effective but also consider the cost of treatment for an individual patient.

The Himmelfarb Library disseminates information about the Affordable Care Act through their institutional repository. Their Health Sciences Research Commons website (http://hsrc.himmelfarb.gwu.edu/) records citations to published articles by GW faculty in the schools of Medicine and Health Sciences, Public Health, and Nursing. Some of the health policy faculty helped draft sections of the Affordable Care Act, and they have written articles about the effects of the law and its implementation. Librarians scan MEDLINE to identify articles by GW faculty to record in the repository.

MICHELLE KRAFT, MSLS

Senior medical librarian
Cleveland Clinic Alumni Library, Cleveland, Ohio
Website: http://kraftylibrarian.com

Librarian Advocate at a Glance

- Teaches continuing education classes for hospital librarians on the Affordable Care Act and its impact on hospital libraries
- Advocates for demonstrating the impact of libraries on hospitals budgets, admission rates, and other ACA-related measures

Librarian Advocate Profile

Michelle Kraft works at the Cleveland Clinic Alumni Library, a hospital library located at a multispecialty academic medical center integrating clinical and hospital care with research and education. As a hospital librarian, Michelle emphasizes the importance of "getting a foot in the door" in order to establish successful and innovative programs. She recommends librarians advocate for their services by reversing the elevator speech—find out what the person in the elevator is doing and then determine what librarians can do to support those initiatives and help solve unmet needs.

As an example of an innovative project that directly addressed hospital needs, Cindy Avallone, also of the Cleveland Clinic Alumni Library, worked

Michelle Kraft, Librarian Advocate Profile. Photo courtesy of Michelle Kraft.

with patient education and hospital information technology services to create smart phases designed to integrate quality medical information within electronic health records (EHRs). In addition, Cindy partnered with some of the hospital departments to create specific LibGuides that could in turn be linked to within the EHR. Both of these efforts were designed to address meaningful-use requirements featured in the ACA law.

To encourage other hospital librarians to think creatively about demonstrating their worth, Michelle has been teaching a continuing education class for hospital librarians specifically about the Affordable Care Act and its impact on hospital budgets, readmission rates, and other factors. In her class entitled "The Evolving Librarian: Responding to Changes in the Workplace and Healthcare," she urges hospital librarians to change the goals of their libraries so that they more accurately reflect the goals of the hospital. By directly aligning library goals with hospital goals, hospital librarians can demonstrate to hospital administration that they are making a difference using metrics that are most meaningful to that group. Michelle adds, "It's not necessarily changing our focus; it's changing how we present our focus and how our library resources are being used." Hospital librarians need to present their statistics in a way that hospital administrators understand. It is a matter of changing one's perspective toward first looking at how the hospital is approaching goals and then assessing how the library fits in there.

Hospital librarians could use the following questions as a model of this thought process: How can hospital librarians help with patient readmission? Who are the players involved (e.g., patients, nurses, physicians)? How can we measure our help? To answer these questions, hospital librarians could work directly with hospital administration on the specific steps they are taking to reduce readmission rates.

Michelle offers another scalable strategy—for every search strategy or article that a hospital librarian sends out, he or she could feature a Survey-Monkey link at the bottom labeled "Please let me know how I am doing and how this is impacting your work." A short survey could be developed that would get at the question of how the librarian's work directly impacts patient care. Even if not everyone fills out the survey, those who do contribute may provide the hospital librarian with some quantifiable outcome information.

Michelle also recommends serving on hospital committees to see how one's institution is being impacted by the ACA. From these discussions a hospital librarian can pick one or two low-hanging fruits to begin their initiatives targeted to meet these needs. As a librarian advocate, Michelle offers concrete strategies that assist librarians in targeting their efforts where they most directly meet patrons' needs.

APPENDIX: SEMISTRUCTURED INTERVIEW GUIDE/PROTOCOL

- This study is designed to collect information about librarians' experiences meeting Affordable Care Act and health insurance information needs. The results may be presented at professional conferences and published in relevant journals or books. Your participation is voluntary and most appreciated. Do you consent to participate in this study?
- First, could you tell me a little bit about the library that you work in and your role there?

- Now, could you tell me a little bit about your experiences meeting Afford-able Care Act and/or health insurance information needs?
- Interview follow-up question: Did it seem that [one of these categories] was more frequent than others? Was there a typical kind of patron looking for health insurance information?
- Interview follow-up question: Can you please describe one of the Afford-able Care Act or health insurance reference questions/interviews you re-sponded to? Perhaps one that stands out to you?
- Possible probing questions may inquire after the patron, the medium in which it was conducted (e.g., face-to-face, email, phone), and recom-mended resources.
- Would you describe it as successful? If so, why?
- Did you participate in any training on this topic? Can you tell me how you found out about these training opportunities? How helpful did you find them?
- Thank you so much for your time today!

Chapter Seven

Recommended Affordable Care Act Information Resources for Consumers

Kelli Ham, Michele Malloy, and Brenda M. Linares

As the implementation of the Affordable Care Act (ACA) continues, consumers face a complex informational need for resources to help them make informed choices. Libraries must both understand the potential questions posed by these diverse populations and be aware of quality resources. With high stakes and a lack of authoritative, unbiased print materials, libraries can assist patrons by guiding essential access to web-based resources, including basic information about insurance and the ACA; resources about enrollment processes, deadlines, and requirements; tax-related sources; and population-specific guides and providers.

This chapter will define various information-seeking consumer groups, explain their needs and how we selected objective sources, discuss evaluation tips for all sites, and then list useful resources. Suggested resources will include brief annotations, tips for use, and indications as to which groups may find them most useful. Since web-based resources change rapidly and new sources will be created quickly, supplemental information includes higher-level links to the organizations and suggestions for future resource identification.

ACA CONSUMERS

Many groups are impacted by the ACA and will approach information professionals for support; this chapter guides provision of sources for consumers, while the next chapter focuses on the needs of professionals. For the purposes of this chapter, consumers can include patients, family or caregivers, and the general public. Some consumer groups, such as immigrants, minority populations, and others with specific circumstances, may have distinct questions and needs.

SELECTION OF RESOURCES

Resources in this chapter were gathered through both searches and references to similar resource lists and chosen based on standard evaluation criteria (discussed in the following section). The survey and interviews referred to in chapters 5 and 6 provided a sample of sources employed by health information professionals, and this group was supplemented by the authors. Since individual web pages change often, especially in evolving topic areas, links to top-level websites were chosen more often over more specific pages that will likely change.

EVALUATION TIPS

Since this resource chapter does not aim to provide an exhaustive or comprehensive list, resources other than those included may be appropriate for answering a specific user's questions. As the topic of health insurance provision in the United States evolves, consumers will ask new questions and have access to new resources. Evaluating resources remains an essential skill for both information provider and consumer, due to disparities in the strength of sources. The criteria for evaluating health insurance resources can mirror measures for health and medical information. Below, commonly accepted indicators are listed with notes regarding application to the ACA.

Authority

As a controversial and complex topic, the ACA has prompted creation of many sources. Determining the identity, contact information, and credentials of the resource creators will be essential to evaluation. Note the domain (.gov, .org, .edu, .com) of the site and explain to consumers the indications for authorship.

Accuracy

Consumers require accurate information, especially on this topic. Incorrect information could lead to lapsed or incomplete health care coverage and potential financial liabilities. Seek clear citations, evidence of an editor, and verification from other sources.

Applicability and Coverage

Ensure that the resource's purpose matches the needs of the consumer, and that the site's stated goals actually reflect the information provided. Please review chapter 4 for guidance in conducting a reference interview on this topic. Consider the needs of specific information seekers, and examine reading level, language, and site accessibility and usability. Also make sure that the scope of coverage matches the needs of the consumer.

Objectivity

All topics have the potential for bias, but health care reform can be particularly polarizing and sensational. Both informational and journalistic sources on health care, health insurance, and the ACA can contain explicit or implied bias. Identify the intent, authorship, and goals of the site, and make sure this fits the needs of the user and is as objective as possible. Authoritative governmental sites, though in favor of the ACA, can provide clear directional information for consumers. Some consumers may also want partisan views, and information professionals can guide them toward the strongest options and supplement with balancing sources.

Currency

Some provisions of the ACA and tax implications change each year, so it is vitally important to ensure that the resource or information provided is the most current available. Similarly, insurance options are time sensitive. Librarians should pay attention to important dates throughout the year, such as the enrollment period, tax filing deadlines, and effective dates of year-to-year changes to the law.

RESOURCES

The ACA changed the landscape of health care and created new options for individuals with regard to health insurance coverage. Librarians can expect questions about any aspect of the law, health insurance options, and corresponding tax implications. The following links will provide a core set of resources to answer the most common questions from consumers. This list can also be used as a primer for library staff to prepare in advance for questions about health insurance and the ACA and may serve as a starting point for those wishing to develop LibGuides or other information portals for health insurance information resources.

Healthcare.gov serves as the primary resource for information about the ACA. Currently, it is the official site of the federal government health insurance marketplace for thirty-four states. Over the coming years, librarians can expect changes to the health reform and the corresponding informational resources. While the individual links provided here might change, searches on the topics within authoritative sites should lead to appropriate resources at later dates.

The Basics

On March 23, 2010, President Obama signed legislation that put comprehensive health insurance reforms into place. The law intends to make health care more affordable, easier to obtain, and of a higher quality for individuals, families, and businesses. Key features of the law include protections for consumers, coverage of preventive services, barring insurance companies from denying coverage due to preexisting conditions, and many other aspects. Library users may want to know basic information about the ACA and what it means for them or a family member. The best starting place is Healthcare.gov, the official federal government website (https://www.healthcare.gov/). Even though a number of states operate their own marketplaces, much of the general information on the federal site applies across all states. Another key site is the "Health Insurance" topic page on MedlinePlus, a compilation of current, authoritative resources that can help librarians easily monitor and quickly retrieve relevant information for consumers (http://medlineplus.gov/healthinsurance/).

- "Glossary." The ACA and sweeping health care reform brought a new emphasis on health insurance, including terminology that might be new or confusing to individuals. Healthcare.gov provides a comprehensive A-to-Z listing of terms related to health insurance and the ACA to help make sense of the terminology. Online at https://www.healthcare.gov/glossary/.
- "Quick Guide to the Marketplace." This one-page guide explains the marketplace in simple terms, including information about deadlines, Medicaid and the Children's Health Insurance Plan (CHIP), and current penalties for not having insurance. Online at https://www.healthcare.gov/quick-guide/.
- "About the Law." For quick reference, this at-a-glance overview of key features of the law such as coverage, costs, and care will be helpful for librarians. It also includes a link to the actual text of the law and a year-by-year overview of reforms that will roll out over the next several years. Online at http://www.hhs.gov/healthcare/rights/index.html.
- "Preventive Care." Learn more about preventive services available under the Affordable Care Act, including services for women. Online at http://www.hhs.gov/healthcare/rights/preventive-care/index.html.
- "How to Choose Marketplace Insurance." Many options exist for health plans; this page offers several sections that help individuals learn about

important factors to consider when comparing plans, including the metal tier system, costs, benefits, catastrophic plans, and much more. Online at https://www.healthcare.gov/choose-a-plan/.
- "Marketplace Insurance Categories." Health plan categories are designated by "metal tiers"; this page explains the system in detail. Online at https://www.healthcare.gov/choose-a-plan/plans-categories/.
- "What Marketplace Plans Cover." Under the new law, all health insurance plans must cover the same set of essential benefits, as explained here. Online at https://www.healthcare.gov/coverage/.
- "Screener." Use this simple screener to learn if a user qualifies for a special enrollment period or if they are eligible for Medicaid or CHIP. Online at https://www.healthcare.gov/screener/.
- "What the Insurance Jargon Means for Families" provides an easy-to-follow guide of the various terms used in the marketplace. Online at http://www.fv-ncfpp.org/blog/what-insurance-jargon-means-families/.

Consumer Guides

- "The Health Care Law and You." The Institute of Medicine produced this user-friendly guide about the new law for the 2014–2015 enrollment period. In the event that updated guides have a new URL, search the IOM site for the current version. Online at http://www.iom.edu/4questionsGuide.
- "Know Your Health Insurance." Merck Engage provides an easy-to-understand, interactive guide for consumers. Of special note is the FAQ section, which covers many questions and provides information in simple, understandable language. Online at http://www.merckengage.com/know-yourhealthinsurance/default.aspx.
- "Coverage to Care." This Department of Health and Human Services initiative aims to help newly insured individuals understand their benefits and connect to health care and appropriate preventive services. Librarians can direct users to the "Roadmap to Better Care and a Healthier You," a step-by-step quick reference guide for consumers. Online at http://www.hhs.gov/healthcare/prevention/index.html.
- "Protect Yourself From Fraud." In addition to understanding the new health insurance law, consumers may also be faced with attempts at fraud. To educate consumers, the Centers for Medicare and Medicaid Services (CMS) developed fact sheets in English and Spanish. Online at https://marketplace.cms.gov/outreach-and-education/protect-yourself-from-fraud-in-health-insurance-marketplace.pdf (English) and https://marketplace.cms.gov/outreach-and-education/protect-yourself-from-fraud-in-health-insurance-marketplace-spanish.pdf (Spanish).
- Gruber, Jonathan. *Health Care Reform: What It Is, Why It Is Necessary, How It Works*. New York: Hill and Wang, 2011. This book walks every-

one through a basic understanding of the ACA with illustrations and examples. This is a graphic novel.

- Yagoda, Lisa. *Affordable Care Act for Dummies*. Hoboken, NJ: John Wiley & Sons, 2014. Explains the ACA in basic terminology for everyone and offers key information on enrollment, coverage, and benefits.

Federal and State Exchanges

The ACA allowed states the option of utilizing the federally facilitated exchange, creating a state-run exchange, or a combination of the two as a partnership exchange. The majority of states chose to utilize the federal site, Healthcare.gov. Other states created their own exchanges, some created partnership sites, and some are changing status after the first year of implementation. Librarians must be aware of the status of their own state and how to find information for other states, as the information and procedures may vary. Careful and thorough communication during the reference interview will guide your search and selection of materials for the patron.

If the state for which the patron needs information operates its own exchange, the librarian will be able to provide materials directly from the state site. Expect to find consumer guides, tools, and other resources specific to that state, including directories for local organizations and help with enrollment. Also, state exchange sites may have outreach materials that libraries can use for patron awareness and programming associated with enrollment activities.

- "Get Coverage." A quick tool to find the marketplace in a given state; entering a state provides the marketplace name and a link to the respective site. Online at https://www.healthcare.gov/get-coverage/.
- "The Health Insurance Marketplace." For a quick snapshot of all state exchanges, the IRS provides an up-to-date table listing all of the state exchanges. Toll-free phone numbers and links are included. Online at http://www.irs.gov/Affordable-Care-Act/Individuals-and-Families/The-Health-Insurance-Marketplace.
- "State by State." An interactive map with statistics and information about each state's status and impact is available from the Department of Health and Human Services. Please note: the map does not include links to the actual state sites. Online at http://www.hhs.gov/healthcare/facts/bystate/statebystate.html.
- "Find Local Help." Healthcare.gov created this simple tool that directs individuals to the right starting point for asking questions or enrolling in a health care plan. Anyone who prefers speaking with someone in person can call the hotline at 1-800-318-2596. Online at https://local-help.healthcare.gov and http://www.healthcare.gov/contact-us/.

- "Consumer Assistance Program." CMS provides a very useful directory of consumer assistance programs, other programs, and state agencies for all states, regardless of whether the state participates in the federally facilitated exchange or operates its own exchange. Online at www.cms.gov/ CCIIO/Resources/Consumer-Assistance-Grants/.

Taxes, Penalties, and Deadlines

Health insurance coverage affected U.S. citizens' federal income taxes starting with 2014 federal tax returns. One component of the ACA requires that everyone who can afford health insurance demonstrate coverage or face a penalty. This penalty or fine can be referred to as the individual mandate or individual responsibility payment. Exemptions are available for those who cannot afford health insurance and for other defined circumstances. In the coming years, higher penalties will be phased in to encourage enrollment. Library patrons are accustomed to visiting the library for tax forms and publications; patrons will likely inquire about the tax filing requirements and the individual mandate.

With the availability of tax publications and forms online, libraries have reduced the number of paper forms provided to patrons. However, knowing about the official forms and publications that relate to the new law will remain essential for librarians. Other useful resources include consumer guides about the new law and how it affects an individual's tax situation. Since forms and information will change every year, librarians should go directly to the Internal Revenue Service website (http://irs.gov) and search for "health insurance" or "Affordable Care Act" to find the most current information. In 2015, helpful charts, tools, and an infographic broke down the complex tax issues to help consumers with this new filing requirement.

Another important aspect for library staff involves knowledge of the enrollment periods, deadlines, and triggers for special enrollment periods, which may change from year to year. For coverage in 2015, the open enrollment period ended February 15, but a special enrollment opened because many taxpayers were not aware of the tax implications for not having coverage. For coverage starting in 2016, the open enrollment period is November 1, 2015, through January 31, 2016. Librarians can sign up for alerts from Healthcare.gov or specific state exchanges for news and notifications to stay up to date.

- "Affordable Care Act (ACA) Tax Provisions." The IRS created this section to help individuals and businesses navigate the complex tax information and filing requirements. Online at http://www.irs.gov/Affordable-Care-Act.

- "Health Coverage and Your Federal Income Taxes." Individuals will appreciate an overview of how health insurance affects their taxes. This page provides a simple explanation with links to necessary publications and taxes. Online at https://www.healthcare.gov/taxes/.
- "Tools to Help You Claim the Affordability Exemption and Calculate Your Premium Tax Credit." This page explains the process of claiming the affordability exemption and calculating the premium tax credit. Online at https://www.healthcare.gov/taxes/tools/.
- "The Health Care Law and Your Taxes." IRS Publication 5201 is an easy-to-understand infographic for consumers; the publication explains in simple terms the requirements and all the important terms. Online at http://www.irs.gov/file_source/pub/irs-pdf/p5201.pdf.

Easy-to-Read, Multilingual, and Multimedia Resources

Certain segments of the population will face even greater challenges than the general public. People with low literacy or who do not speak English as their first language will have additional difficulties accessing and understanding written materials, in part because of the complexity of the law and the limited availability of easy-to-read materials (refer to chapter 3 for a more in-depth discussion). Extensive materials exist in Spanish, and other language materials are available to varying degrees; most authoritative sites offer at least some materials in other languages. Healthcare.gov provides some information in more than a dozen languages, and IRS.gov provides online materials in five languages not including English. State exchanges provide materials in the majority of languages spoken within the state. For enrollment help and questions, the federal exchange and state exchanges offer extensive services for people who speak other languages; check the appropriate website for toll-free numbers.

- "Glossary of Health Coverage and Medical Terms." This well-designed glossary from the Centers for Medicare and Medicaid Services is written in simple language and includes illustrations to help make complex terms more understandable. Online at http://www.cms.gov/CCIIO/Resources/Files/Downloads/uniform-glossary-final.pdf.
- "From Coverage to Care Roadmap Videos." For individuals with lower literacy skills, videos are often a good alternative to print materials. As part of the Roadmap, CMS created a YouTube channel with eleven short videos in both English and Spanish that may be helpful for library patrons. Search for the channel "From Coverage to Care" for videos in English and "Cobertura Para Su Salud" for the Spanish versions. Online at https://www.youtube.com/user/HealthCareGov/playlists.

- "Cuidado de Salud (Healthcare.gov)." The Spanish version of Health-care.gov is accessible by going directly to the link or by clicking on the "Español" button. Online at https://www.cuidadodesalud.gov/es/.
- "La Ley de Cuidado de Salud: recursos para los consumidores." The Kaiser Family Foundation created several resources for consumers in Spanish, including the popular YouToons video. Online at http://kff.org/cuidado-de-salud-recursos-para-los-consumidores/.
- "Disposiciones Tributarias de la Ley de Cuidado de Salud a Bajo Precio para Personas Físicas y Familias." The IRS website offers substantial materials related to the ACA in Spanish. Visit the ACA section of the IRS website (see above), then click on the "Español" link or go directly to the link shown here. Online at http://www.irs.gov/Spanish/Disposiciones-Tributarias-de-la-Ley-de-Cuidado-de-Salud-a-Bajo-Precio-para-Personas-F%C3%ADsicas-y-Familias.
- "Taxpayer Assistance Center Office Locator." Online tax information in other languages is limited, but this tool can direct users to IRS Taxpayer Assistance Centers that provide help in more than 150 languages through interpretation services. Online at http://apps.irs.gov/app/officeLocator/index.jsp.
- "Free Tax Help Available from the IRS." This document includes a comprehensive list of free services, including the section titled "Help in Other Languages and Formats." Librarians and patrons will appreciate information about accessing help through YouTube videos, downloadable Braille materials, and multilingual services by phone. Online at http://www.irs.gov/uac/Free-Tax-Help-Available-From-the-IRS-1.

Special Circumstances and Populations

The ACA includes provisions and options for many different groups of people, such as persons with disabilities, immigrant families, pregnant women, LGBT populations, and others. The federal exchange offers applicative information, and each state exchange will provide details relevant to the specific state. In addition, local clinics and other community organizations provide resources and helpful guides for the specific populations they serve. Be sure to visit the resources or directory section of state exchange sites. Provided below are two general resources and one for a specific population as examples.

- Healthcare.gov serves a good starting point when seeking information for immigrants, persons with disabilities, military veterans, same-sex couples, and a variety of other populations. See a list of help pages by looking under the "Coverage for . . ." heading. Online at https://www.healthcare.gov/get-answers/.

- "Special Populations." The Centers for Medicare and Medicaid Services provide an extensive list of resources; librarians can find helpful resources on this page for numerous special populations, including minorities, the homeless, refugees, young people, and incarcerated persons. Online at https://marketplace.cms.gov/outreach-and-education/special-populations.html.
- "The Affordable Care Act and Families with Parents Who Are LGBT: Everything You Need to Know." The Family Equality Council explains the features of the ACA that benefit families with LGBT parents, including affordability, nondiscrimination, and coverage for preexisting conditions. Online at http://www.familyequality.org/get_informed/advocacy/know_your_rights/affordable_care_act_guide/.

Instead of compiling an exhaustive and soon outdated list of currently useful resources, this chapter guides information professionals through potential users' needs and the process of identifying and evaluating tools, and then highlights examples from different categories. Please use this guide as a starting point in the provision of authoritative and useful ACA information for your specific communities. As hubs of public information, libraries can further serve consumers by updating local resource lists, collaborating with colleagues, and sharing evolving questions and tools.

Chapter Eight

Recommended Affordable Care Act Information Resources for Practitioners

Michele Malloy and Brenda M. Linares

Provision of appropriate and authoritative resources regarding the Affordable Care Act (ACA) and health insurance has become increasingly important for information professionals. The previous chapter outlined tools for consumers, while this chapter focuses on the concerns and needs of professionals involved in health care. Professionals, who provide and support care for consumers, have distinct informational needs beyond practical lay resources.

This chapter will define various professional roles and their overlapping but unique resource needs. Following last chapter's pattern, selection and evaluation tips are provided with a focus on the information needs of practitioners, followed by recommended resources. These tools fall into categories that may be applicable to more than one professional group: research, government, law, statistics, and works from organizations or associations. Since the resources and categories are not exhaustive, libraries are encouraged to tailor their own research guides to the evolving needs of their patrons, especially as the topic of health reform and insurance develops.

ACA PROFESSIONALS

Health professionals, as providers and researchers involved in health care, have been doubly impacted by the ACA. Not only do they face questions from their positions as consumers and in support of patients, but they also seek to understand changes in a research and organizational context. For consumer-driven questions, the previous chapter supports both individual decision making and patient support; this chapter addresses policy, organizational, and practice concerns. Though many groups of professionals may study the ACA, the general categories below summarize those in health care most likely to seek health-focused information.

Practitioners

Practitioners, including physicians, nurses, pharmacists, allied health professionals, technicians, and many other essential providers, interact with patients on a daily basis. Accordingly, they want to develop their knowledge and understanding of how the ACA may change health care from daily patient interactions to financial and organizational implications. These information seekers often desire content specific to their specialty, geographical area, and practice type. They may have backgrounds in research or policy, or they may prefer practical and broad overviews.

Researchers

As the ACA implementation progresses, our health care system will experience a wide range of changes, and researchers study this progress. Some focus on changes in quality and provision of care, while others examine financial models or perceptions of professionals and patients. This group will focus on sources beyond informational web overviews and will need research support surrounding complex searches of academic and methodologically sound studies.

Health Policy Makers and Analysts

Policy specialists from academic, governmental, and organizational fields have wide informational needs. Though they appreciate sound research content, they also seek legal analysis, statistical reports, programmatic examples, and reports of public perception and needs.

Health Care Administrators and Organizations

As they adapt to the ACA and subsequent changes in insurance provision, health care organizations need a variety of informational sources. Some will seek models from other organizations, implement continuing education programs for their staff, or integrate patient education and support systems.

Insurance Providers and Small Businesses

Though they may seek information from an internal or centralized source, companies either providing or facilitating insurance provision will also have informational needs. Small businesses need support understanding legal requirements and options, while insurance providers seek data on enrollment and consumer trends.

Journalists

With controversy and misinformation sometimes clouding public understanding of the ACA, journalists need clarification of details not only about the actual law, but about health care or insurance procedures and terminology.

Librarians and Information Professionals

As providers of information to both consumers and professionals, librarians need a broad view of the spectrum of resources in order to best serve all populations.

SELECTION OF RESOURCES

Resources in this chapter were gathered through both searches and references to similar resource lists, and chosen based on standard evaluation criteria. The survey and interviews referred to in chapters 5 and 6 provided a sample of sources employed by health information professionals, and this group was supplemented by the authors. Since individual web pages change often, especially in evolving topic areas, links to top-level websites were chosen more often over more specific pages that will likely change. Especially when discussing resources for researchers, we focused more on search strategies than on actual results.

EVALUATION TIPS

Since this resource chapter does not aim to provide a comprehensive list, resources other than those included may be appropriate for answering a specific user's questions. As the topic of health insurance provision in the United States evolves, professionals will ask new questions and have access to new resources. Evaluating resources remains an essential skill for both information provider and consumer, due to disparities in the strength of sources. The criteria for evaluating health insurance resources can mirror measures for health and medical information. Below, commonly accepted indicators are listed with notes regarding application to the ACA.

Authority

As a controversial and complex topic, the ACA has prompted creation of many sources. Determining the identity, contact information, and credentials of the resource creators will be essential to evaluation. Note the domain (.gov, .org, .edu, .com) of the site and explain to professionals the indications for authorship. Certain professionals may prefer only peer-reviewed works, governmental sources, or items created by their professional organization.

Accuracy

Professionals require accurate information, especially on this topic. Incorrect information could lead to misinformed policies or practice and potential financial liabilities. Seek clear citations, evidence of an editor, and verification from other sources.

Applicability and Coverage

Ensure that the resource's purpose matches the needs of the professional, and that the site's stated goals actually reflect the information provided. Please review chapter 4 for guidance in conducting a reference interview on this topic. Consider the needs of specific information seekers, and make sure that the scope of coverage matches the needs of the consumer.

Objectivity

All topics have the potential for bias, but health care reform can be particularly polarizing and sensational. Both informational and journalistic sources on health care, health insurance, and the ACA can contain explicit or implied bias. Identify the intent, authorship, and goals of the site, and make sure this fits the needs of the user and is as objective as possible. Authoritative governmental sites, though in favor of ACA, can provide clear directional information. Some professionals may also want partisan views, and information professionals can guide them toward the strongest options and supplement with balancing sources. For those engaged in research, prioritize results that offer clearly presented and appropriate methods.

Currency

Some provisions of the ACA and tax implications change each year, so it is vitally important to ensure that the resource or information provided is the most current available. Similarly, insurance options are time sensitive. Librarians should pay attention to important dates throughout the year, such as the enrollment period, tax filing deadlines, and effective dates of year-to-year changes to the law.

RESOURCES

Professionals may seek library assistance in identifying appropriate resources to support a variety of ACA-related work. Practitioners, researchers, policy makers, and others listed earlier in this chapter have a variety of needs. In this section, we categorize basic suggestions by resource type rather than role since these needs will overlap. Libraries serving specific populations can expand resource lists appropriately and identify new tools by delving more deeply into the general categories and further investigating key websites. For basic authoritative information, professionals should also be familiar with the selected consumer sources described in the previous chapter. Healthcare.gov serves as the official governmental website for the ACA and can be a prime background resource for all audiences.

Research Sources

As ACA implementation impacts the U.S. health care system, researchers will continue to study and measure a variety of topics under this umbrella. Within the health sphere, governmental, educational, and organizational websites provide raw data and analysis. Additionally, selected databases such as MEDLINE, CINAHL, and PsycINFO allow for specialized searching within the peer-reviewed literature. Researchers in these areas should also supplement by investigating topical databases in economics, public policy, sociology, and government.

The National Library of Medicine (NLM) provides a number of key research resources for professionals investigating the ACA:

- PubMed MEDLINE, the primary biomedical database provided by the National Library of Medicine, allows researchers to locate peer-reviewed articles on the Affordable Care Act and associated issues. To support searchers, Medical Subject Headings (MeSH) have been developed. Key MeSH terms include "Patient Protection and Affordable Care Act," "National Health Insurance, United States," and "Health Care Reform." Examining the entry terms and MeSH organizational structure of the main heading "Patient Protection and Affordable Care Act" (http://www.ncbi.nlm.nih.gov/mesh/68058991) allows professionals to gather related terms for other searches, understand the scope, and select appropriate subheadings for searches. Online at http://www.ncbi.nlm.nih.gov/pubmed/

- Bookshelf, allowing free access to online health care books, includes a number of ACA titles. Online at http://www.ncbi.nlm.nih.gov/books/.
- PubMed Central, NLM's free public archive of full-text journal literature, can be searched for ACA-related articles. Online at http://www.ncbi.nlm.nih.gov/pmc/.

Additionally, other targeted websites offer datasets and information that will help professionals to understand and investigate the ACA. Selected examples are presented below.

- "Health and Dental Plan Datasets for Researchers and Issuers." Health-care.gov includes downloadable datasets for researchers, allowing them to analyze the raw data about qualified health plans. Online at https://www.healthcare.gov/health-and-dental-plan-datasets-for-researchers-and-issuers/.
- "Affordable Care Act Research Briefs." The Office of the Assistant Secretary for Planning and Evaluation created this group of research and issue briefs analyzing the ACA. Online at http://www.aspe.hhs.gov/health/reports/2012/ACA-Research/index.cfm.
- The Institute of Medicine has held workshops and written reports and briefs about the impacts of the ACA, and will continue to produce useful work on the topic. Professionals should search their site for keywords such as "affordable care act." Online at https://www.iom.edu/.

Governmental Sources

The ACA has caused significant changes on the federal and state level, and to support these changes, the U.S. government provides a great deal of information for public and professional entities. Information comes from a variety of governmental agencies and sites; direct links are provided in this section, and professionals are encouraged to investigate higher-level sites for updates and new topics.

- "Affordable Care Act." The Congressional Budget Office provides analysis of the effects of the Act under current law and the effects of proposed changes to the law. Online at https://www.cbo.gov/topics/health-care/affordable-care-act.
- "HealthCare." The U.S. Department of Health and Human Services is the U.S. government's principal agency for protecting the health of all Americans, and they dedicate this section of the website to providing information about the ACA. The "Facts and Features" tab may be especially helpful to professionals. Online at http://www.hhs.gov/healthcare/.

- "Affordable Care Act and HRSA Programs." Provides useful information on decision making and partnering with community health centers to educate consumers. The "Provider Tool Kit" resources will be a key section for professionals. Online at http://www.hrsa.gov/affordablecareact/.
- "Health Insurance." MedlinePlus lists quality resources links about health insurance and the Affordable Care Act. Online at http://www.nlm.nih.gov/medlineplus/healthinsurance.html.
- "Health Insurance." The U.S. Census Bureau collects health insurance data using three national surveys: the Current Population Survey's Annual Social and Economic Supplement (CPS ASEC), the American Community Survey (ACS), and the Survey of Income and Program Participation (SIPP). Online at http://www.census.gov/hhes/www/hlthins/.
- "Affordable Care Act Tax Provisions for Employers." The IRS's specialized website describes small- and large-employer differences and what each group needs to know about the ACA. Employer benefits, opportunities, and requirements are dependent upon the employer's size and the applicable rules, which are showcased on this site. Online at http://www.irs.gov/Affordable-Care-Act/Employers.
- "U.S. Department of Labor: Affordable Care Act." The U.S. Department of Labor has created a centralized site covering basic issues that employers need to be aware of on this topic. Online at http://www.dol.gov/ebsa/healthreform/.
- "Become a Champion for Coverage." From the health insurance marketplace, this site promotes the idea of becoming a champion and ensuring that Americans can get the care they need, when they need it, at a price they can afford. It also provides information on outreach and education. Online at https://marketplace.cms.gov/technical-assistance-resources/assister-programs/champion.html.
- "From Coverage to Care." Provides written resources and videos to aid individuals in understanding their benefits and connecting to primary-care and the preventive services that are right for them, so they can live a long and healthy life. Online at http://marketplace.cms.gov/technical-assistance-resources/c2c.html.
- The National Network of Libraries of Medicine provides health professionals and the general public with health information resources and services. Their regional ACA guides group useful key resources for professionals and consumers: Greater Midwest Region: http://nnlm.gov/gmr/outreach/aca; MidContinental Region: http://nnlm.gov/mcr/resources/aca.html; Middle Atlantic Region: http://guides.nnlm.gov/mar_aca; New England Region: http://nnlm.gov/ner/training/aca.html; Pacific Northwest Region: http://nnlm.gov/pnr/ACA.html; Pacific Southwest Region: http://guides.nnlm.gov/psr/aca; South Central Region: http://nnlm.gov/scr/out-

reach/aca.html; and Southeastern/Atlantic Region: http://guides.nnlm.gov/sea/ACA.

Legal Sources

Professionals may be interested in the multiple legal implications of the ACA. This section showcases basic legal information via online resources and books. For more in-depth legal investigation, encourage professionals to interact with law libraries.

- "About the Law." The Department of Health and Human Services site outlines key features and information about the law. It also provides vital information with a year-by-year breakdown. Online at http://www.hhs.gov/healthcare/rights/.
- "H.R.3590: Patient Protection and Affordable Care Act." Congress.gov serves as a public portal to the bill summary, action history, and versions of the full text. Online at https://www.congress.gov/bill/111th-congress/house-bill/3590.
- "A Legislative History of the Affordable Care Act: How Legislative Procedure Shapes Legislative History." The American Association of Law Libraries published this helpful legislative history as a reference. Online at http://www.aallnet.org/mm/Publications/llj/LLJ-Archives/Vol-105/no-2/2013-7.pdf.
- "Consumer Reports: Health Law Helper." An informational tool designed for individual consumers, this site incorporates the best information *Consumer Reports* has about the law's impact on consumers. Online at https://www.healthlawhelper.org/.
- Gans, David H. *Religious Liberties for Corporations? Hobby Lobby, the Affordable Care Act, and the Constitution.* New York: Palgrave Macmillan, 2014. This book provides a comprehensive analysis of the issues and the cases brought to the U.S. Supreme Court.
- Jost, Timothy S. *The Patient Protection and Affordable Care Act and the Health Care and Education Reconciliation Act of 2010.* New Providence, NJ: LexisNexis, 2010. This work overviews information about the ACA law and its relation to patients.
- Auten, Meredith S., Ron Chapman Jr., Tom Christina, Stephen M. Goodman, Stephen G. Prom, and Bruce Platt. *Understanding the Health Care Reform Bill: An Immediate Look at the Potential Impact of the Patient Protection and Affordable Care Act.* Aspatore Special Report. N.p.: Thomson West, 2014.

Sources from Organizations, Associations, and Others

Many organizations compile useful information about the Affordable Care Act and its implications for patients, doctors, nurses, and other health care providers. This chapter provides a brief list of some of those organizations and associations, and libraries can supplement this list with other groups appropriate to the specific professional.

- "Health Reform." The Kaiser Family Foundation organizes this topic page dedicated to overviews and trends involving health care reform. Statistical highlights of this source include the "State Health Facts" (http://kff.org/state-category/health-reform/). Online at http://kff.org/health-reform/.
- "The Patient Protection and Affordable Care Act." The Brookings Institution, as a nonprofit provider of policy research, overviews issues involving the ACA. Online at http://www.brookings.edu/research/topics/affordable-care-act.
- "Advocacy Topics: Affordable Care Act." The American Medical Association hosts tips on how physicians can assist their patients in acquiring health insurance. "Related Links" will be helpful for physicians. Online at http://www.ama-assn.org/ama/pub/advocacy/topics/affordable-care-act.page.
- "Get Enrolled!" The American Hospital Association provides information on getting enrolled, with additional information such as tool kits and national and state resources. Online at http://www.aha.org/advocacy-issues/initiatives/enroll/index.shtml.
- "Health Care Reform." The American Nursing Association guides nursing professionals to policy and advocacy resources about the ACA and health care reform. Online at http://www.nursingworld.org/healthcarereform.
- "Health Reform." The American Public Health Association provides an overview of the ACA for public health professionals, with useful FAQs and key ACA resources. Online at https://www.apha.org/topics-and-issues/health-reform.
- "Affordable Care Act." The American Library Association maintains a topic page for the ACA, including information on the role of libraries and a list of key resources. Online at http://www.ala.org/tools/affordable-care-act.
- "State Actions to Address Health Insurance Exchanges." The National Conference of State Legislatures hosts a comprehensive page with current information about each state's marketplace/exchange implementation, including a state-by-state breakdown of important facts and reported enrollment figures for the most recent period. Online at http://www.ncsl.org/research/health/state-actions-to-implement-the-health-benefit.aspx.

- "Staterefor(u)m." An initiative of the National Academy for State Health Policy funded by the Robert Wood Johnson Foundation, this is an online network for health reform implementation. Online at https://www.statereforum.org.
- Goldsmith, Francisca. *Libraries and the Affordable Care Act: Helping Understand Health-Care Options*. Chicago: American Library Association, 2014. Organized reference tool to enable libraries to serve both consumers and professionals.
- Gruber, Jonathan. *Health Care Reform: What It Is, Why It Is Necessary, How It Works*. New York: Hill and Wang, 2011. This book walks everyone through a basic understanding of the ACA with illustrations and examples.
- Thompson, Tamara. *The Affordable Care Act*. Farmington Hills, MI: Greenhaven Press, 2015. This book explores the pros and cons of the Affordable Care Act, including who benefits and how the economy is affected.
- Yagoda, Lisa. *Affordable Care Act for Dummies*. Hoboken, NJ: John Wiley & Sons, 2014. Explains the ACA in basic terminology for everyone and offers key information on enrollment, coverage, and benefits.

CONCLUSION

Professional needs for ACA resources will continue to evolve as health care law influences practice. By addressing core groups of professional information seekers and their current and projected needs, this chapter seeks to guide information providers as they create a support system for researchers, health care providers, and other professionals. The resources and tips outlined above provide a starting point for information providers, and librarians should continually supplement resources according to patron needs and newly available tools.

Index

About the Editor

Emily Vardell, MLS, is a doctoral student and teaching fellow at the School of Information and Library Science (SILS) at the University of North Carolina, Chapel Hill. Her research interests focus on health information behavior, particularly health insurance literacy and decision-making. As a teaching fellow, she has served as the instructor of record for graduate-level courses on health sciences information and information resources and services. Emily was the director for reference and education at the Louis Calder Medical Library at the University of Miami and earned her master's of library science from Texas Woman's University in 2007 as a distance education student while working as a Fulbright scholar in Austria. She began her medical librarian career as a National Library of Medicine associate fellow. Emily is an active member of the Medical Library Association (MLA), and has served as chair of the MLA Public Health/Health Administration Section and chair-designate of the MLA Professional Recruitment and Retention Committee. She is a recipient of the Association for Information Science and Technology (ASIS&T) New Leaders Award and is active in the ASIS&T Health Informatics Special Interest Group. She is the online updates column editor for *Medical Reference Services Quarterly*, where she reviews a health-related database each quarter.